ISRAELI WAR MACHINE

ISRAELI WAR MACHINE

HAMLYN

London New York Sydney Toronto

Contents

A Quarto Book

Published by the
Hamlyn Publishing Group Limited
London New York Sydney Toronto
Astronaut House, Feltham,
Middlesex, England

Copyright © 1983 Quarto
Publishing Limited
All rights reserved. No part of this
publication may be reproduced, stored in
a retrieval system, or transmitted in any
form or by any means, electronic,
mechanical, photocopying, recording, or
otherwise, without the permission of the
Hamlyn Publishing Group Limited and
the copyright holder.

ISBN 0 600 385 140

This book was designed and produced
by Quarto Publishing Limited, 32 Kingly
Court, London W1

Maps and diagrams
© QED Publishing Ltd, London
Aircraft profiles
© Pilot Press, Bromley, Kent
Tank illustrations by Nick Gibbard and
Profile Books
Photographs from the collections of John
Topham Picture Library, Edenbridge,
Kent; Gamma, Paris; S Peltz; Frank
Spooner Pictures, London; Aviation
Photographs, Swindon, UK; John Frost
Newspaper Library, Barnet, UK.

Filmset by QV Typesetting, London
Color origination by
Rodney Howe Ltd, London
Black-and-white origination by Speedlith
Photo Litho Ltd, Manchester
Printed in Hong Kong
by Leefung Asco Printers Ltd

Forging the Machine

IN SOMETHING LIKE 30 YEARS the Israeli Armed Forces have apparently progressed from nothing to being one of the most efficient and battle-hardened forces in the world and, though they have suffered setbacks, they have never suffered defeat. Their motivation is not hard to find — either they win or their nation is destroyed, with Israel simply ceasing to exist as a political entity. Motivation alone, however, does not build armies, so the question remains as to how this standard was reached in such a relatively short time?

In fact, if the record is examined closely, it becomes clear that the Israeli Army has been in existence, in one form or another and to a greater or lesser degree, for almost a century. Although during that time it has frequently been concealed or camouflaged, it has built up a tradition and a background which has created an immense *ésprit de corps* in its present members, and it is worth looking at its gestation in order to see what that background is.

Jewish attempts to return to or remain in the Holy Land have gone on without interruption for almost two millenia, and in spite of every obstacle there has always been some Jewish presence there throughout the ages. In the 1880s, the movement to return gained considerable momentum, largely fuelled by the massive series of pogroms in Russia after 1882. This led to a surge of emigration to other parts of Europe, the USA, and, in smaller numbers, back to the Holy Land. The failure of the 1905 Revolution in Russia gave

In the beginning Until Turkish defeat in 1918, Palestine was part of the Turkish Empire. To protect themselves, the early Jewish settlers organized their first defence force — Hashomer. Armed with rifles and daggers, and with ammunition belts slung around their shoulders, a group of Hashomer stand ready for action at Mes'ha, Galilee, in 1904 **(right)**. Israel Shoat, Hashomer's first commander, stands in the center, with wide-brimmed hat and up-turned collar. With the coming of world war, Zionism increased its strength, with British support. Dr Chaim Weizmann, chairman of the Zionist Commission, arrives at British headquarters in Palestine **(below)**.

Liberation Jewish volunteers **(right)** flocked to the British colors during General Allenby's Palestine campaign, spurred on by the promise of a 'national home' after British victory. They were formed into the Jewish Regiment, under the command of Lt-Colonel JH Patterson **(above)**, though, by the time they saw action, Turkish resistance was collapsing **(top)**. Allenby's triumphs included the capture of Jerusalem, which he is seen leaving by the Jaffa gate **(bottom right)**.

further impulsion to the movement and brought many more emigrants to Palestine, then under Turkish rule.

Irrespective of the antecedents of the emigrants, their principal hope in Palestine was agriculture, and farm communities sprang up. These were obvious targets for looting and murdering marauders, and there was little help to be got from the Turkish administration which was either hopelessly corrupt, hopelessly ineffectual, or both. The salvation lay in the Jews' own hands, and they rapidly formed self-defence forces. These began as mere watchmen, but it was soon obvious that their effectiveness was improved by a leavening of aggressive action against known bandits. The influx of Russian Jews experienced in defending themselves that followed the 1905 revolution increased the efficiency of the self-defence force to the point where it assumed a more formal structure and in 1907 it became Hashomer, the Jewish Watchmens Association, whose sub-units were given the specific role of protecting outposts and farm settlements.

Hashomer operated successfully for several years, even into the years of the First World War. Then the British Army arrived to give battle to the Turks and their German allies in the Mesopotamian theater, eventually establishing a battle front in Palestine. The Jewish community asked to help in the liberation of the country and, after long negotiation, this was agreed. The first move by the British was to call for Jewish volunteers in Britain in 1917, train and equip them, and send two battalions out to Palestine in 1918. These, though officially known as The Jewish Regiment, formed the 38th and 42nd Battalions of the Royal Fusiliers, commanded by Lt. Col JH Patterson. Upon arrival in Palestine, the regiment's numbers were increased by local voluntary reinforcements and by a large body of volunteers from the USA who, having heard of the formation of the regiment, made their way to Palestine in order to join it. In September 1918 the regiment formed part of General Allenby's forces in his final attack against the Germano-Turkish position in the Jordan valley. It captured the east bank of the Jordan

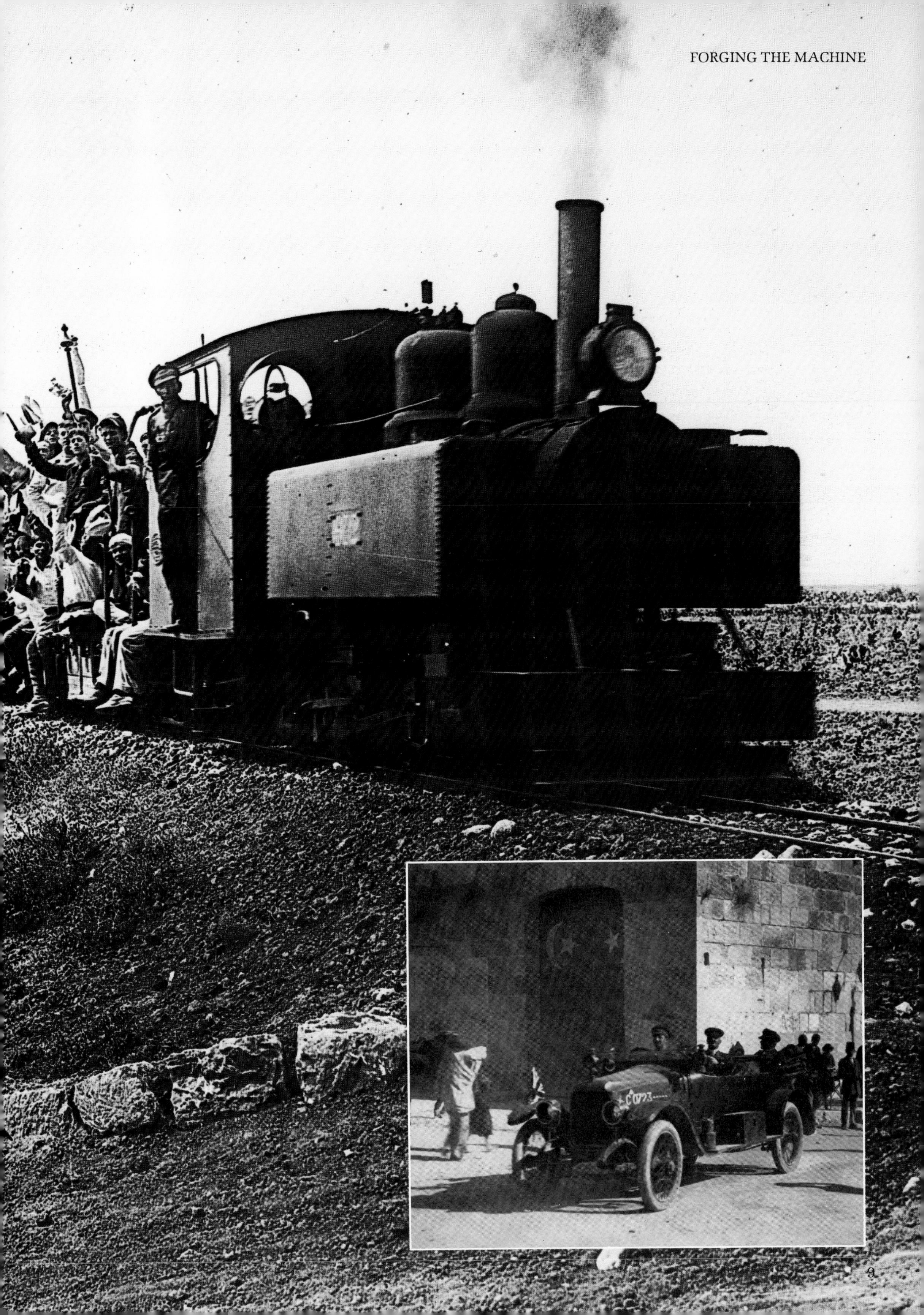

British sympathy Arthur James Balfour **(below)** British cabinet minister during the First World War, promulgated the Balfour Declaration, which pledged British support for a Jewish 'national home' in Palestine. After the war, however, the British found themselves holding the ring between Jew and Arab under a League of Nations mandate.

and advanced well beyond the river before the general collapse of both German and Turkish empires brought the campaign to an end. General Allenby's final despatch spoke highly of the 'Jewish Legion', which had fought extremely well throughout the campaign, the success of their operations leading to more volunteers coming forward until the force finally had a strength of about 6,000 men.

Following the armistice, the foreign volunteers were demobilized and returned to their own countries. The remaining locally-enlisted personnel were formed into the First Judean Battalion and moved to an isolated camp near the Sinai border, because of British fears of a conflict breaking out between them and various Arab elements. In early 1921, however, there was an outburst of anti-Jewish activity by Arabs in Jaffa, and the first battalion, taking matters into its own hands, marched there to protect the Jewish population. Though the British command privately sympathised with the action, the fact remained that troops could not be permitted to take themselves off and into battle as they fancied, and after some debate the battalion was disbanded in May 1921.

The Balfour Declaration of 1917, which stated that Britain regarded Palestine as the Jewish 'national home' increased immigration from troubled post-war Europe and the number of Arab attacks against Jews, notably in Jerusalem and Jaffa, increased as a direct consequence. These made it obvious that self-defence was still a vital factor in the planning of the new Jewish state. Hashomer was no longer sufficient to provide the necessary protection, and a number of ex-Jewish battalion soldiers now proposed its disbandment and replacement by a form of mili-

tia. Every able-bodied Jewish male in Palestine automatically would be a member, to be called upon for duty as and when required. The new militia was to be a clandestine organisation, since neither the Arabs nor the British administration would be willing to see an overt armed levy in existence. The idea was accepted, and Hagana — the word simply means Defence — came into being.

The following years showed the wisdom of setting up Hagana, since Arab attacks on Jewish settlers, with the consequent murder, pillage and looting, intensified. The Jewish response was to strengthen Hagana, ensuring its members were adequately trained, weapons procured and also putting the force to good use in protecting outlying settlements and providing protective screens behind which new ones could be founded.

In 1936 the character of the Arab attacks changed. From isolated incidents carried out by individual bands of brigands, they became concerted assaults by organized groups, and in the face of this Hagana had to change tactics. Hitherto policy had simply been to defend settlements and families, but, with the growing power and mobility of the Arabs, the view that attack might be the best form of defence began to take shape. Obviously the attacker always holds the initiative, and the defender is always forced to respond to the attacker's tune. By adopting an offensive posture, the Arabs could be thrown off-balance and thus the idea of the 'pre-emptive strike' can be said to have evolved. This evolution was considerably assisted by the arrival in Palestine in 1938 of Captain Orde Wingate, a somewhat eccentric British officer with a profound faith in the Zionist cause. Wingate soon began spending his off-duty hours training Hagana units, his involvement with Hagana growing to the point where he actually led night raids against Arab groups in Galilee with a high degree of success. Whilst the regular groupment of Hagana was still of local voluntary groups of militia, called out as necessary, Wingate's 'Night Squads' became regular full-time units, in a permanent state of trained readiness and held as a sort of strategic reserve to be thrown in wherever Arab aggression threatened to become too much for the local force.

It should be stressed that, though Hagana, at this time, was a clandestine organisation, it was far from being a collection of ill-disciplined irregulars. It came under the firm control of the Jewish Agency and the National Council, and its stated purpose was not simply to fight as its fancy took it, but to act as the shield of the Zionist state and cause. Hagana prided itself on this, and on the fact that, except in the case of the Night Squads in 1938-9, it rarely made the first move and was never guilty of aggression. Unfortunately this attitude was somewhat compromised by the activ-

The first Hagana As tension between Jew and Arab rose during the 1930s, Hagana, the Jewish armed militia, was formed. The British saw the organization as subversive, but their attitude was to change with the coming of the Second World War. The Hagana members **(above)** soon found themselves members of the Jewish Settlement Police **(right)**, Palestine's official Home Guard.

Unconventional leader
Charles Orde Wingate
(above), a British regular
with Zionist sympathies,
helped in the training of
Hagana, turning it from a
defence force into one able
and willing to attack.

Against Nazism Jewish involvement in the battle against Hitler's Germany took many forms. In Palestine, recruits were quick to volunteer for the British Army **(top left)**, though at first they were not allowed to fight. Eventually, an all-Jewish Brigade, here seen on parade, was formed **(center left)**, while the Jewish Settlement Police **(center right and bottom)** were the Home Guard in the event of a Nazi breakthrough. Many members of both forces put their training to good use after the war in the struggle for independence.

ities of less responsible, equally clandestine, organizations, who were not averse to retaliation, revenge and the tactics of the vendetta. These unluckily became confused with Hagana in foreign minds.

When the Second World War broke out, the National Council approached the British authorities and offered to raise a force of troops; the unspoken fact behind the offer was that this would mean simply embodying the Hagana and putting it into British uniform. But the British, as always anxious to preserve an uneasy balance between Jew and Arab in Palestine, were reluctant to take up the offer. No similar offer of assistance had come from the Arabs, and it was felt that the acceptance of a Jewish force would leave the British open to accusations of partiality from the Arabs and their supporters. In order to disarm such opposition, the British countered with a suggestion that Jews enlist into non-combatant forces, such as medical units.

This non-combatant role proved successful, so, as the situation in the Middle East slowly deteriorated in 1940-41, the British finally agreed to accept Jewish volunteers for fighting units. At first recruitment was to be strictly controlled so that the number of Jews enlisted balanced the number of Arabs, but since comparatively few Arabs appeared at the recruiting offices, this quota system was quietly abandoned. In 1941 several Jewish battalions were formed, among them the Palmach (Shock Troops). These saw service in Syria against the Vichy French forces and in other Middle Eastern theaters of war.

By 1944 the efficiency of the Jewish soldier was beyond doubt, and a complete Jewish Brigade Group was formed to fight with the British Eighth Army in Northern Italy. This formation, some 27,000 strong, contained a high proportion of ex-Hagana personnel, and was to have crucial significance in the establishment of the Israeli Army in the years to come. Hitherto the members of Hagana had trained simply as basic infantry soldiers, proficient with the rifle and light machine gun, familiar with their own locality and capable of performing relatively simple tactical manoeuvers, such as patrolling, point defence, minor ambushes and co-ordinated company strength attacks. But the intensive training received from British instructors covered every field of military expertise; it included training in the handling of artillery and armor, the technicalities and tactics of parachuting, commando raiding, military engineering, logistics, staff work, planning, tactics, manoeuver and communications. All these and many other specialities were digested by the Jewish Brigade to form a solid foundation for the future. In the opinion of many of the members of the brigade, had not the British trained them so well in the war years, the

Israeli Army might well have been defeated in its first tests after the achievement of statehood.

With the surrender of the Axis in 1945, the Jewish Brigade, enlisted for the duration of the war, was disbanded and its members returned to civilian life. Immediately they picked up the broken threads of their Hagana membership and infused Hagana with a new organization and sense of purpose. The Palmach shock unit was retained in being as a full-time force, though its membership went through a constant change as individuals performed a period of service and then returned into their semi-militia status, going back to their civilian occupations. Palmach's nominal strength was just over 2,000, with an increasing reserve contingent made up of those who had been trained and released. The rest of Hagana numbered about 32,000, split between two sections — the field army and the garrison army. The former consisted of young men charged with the performance of offensive operations within their local area; they trained regularly, during week-ends and holidays, and were an efficient force. The latter, composed of both men and women in a complete basis of equality, were nominated to defensive positions around their settlements in the event of hostilities.

In order to facilitate the command process, the country was divided into three urban commands — Tel Aviv, Haifa and Jerusalem — and three rural commands — north, central and south. These areas were demarcated in such a way as to make each one self-sufficient, meaning that the commanders would have sufficient strength to carry out operations within their own areas without having to call for assistance from other commands.

Underlying and buttressing this organization, was a vast intelligence-gathering network. Primarily this watched and monitored the two principal influences in Palestine, the British forces stationed there to support the British administration, and the Arab irregulars and guerillas, who were maintaining their pressure against the Jews by raiding and random terrorism. In addition there were Hagana agents outside Israel, notably in the various countries of the Middle East where their role was to secure any information that might throw light on the likely reactions to various Jewish proposals and also give some indications of how the various Arab countries would react when the state of Israel was officially proclaimed. Finally, there were Hagana agents charged with keeping watch on the two most notorious Jewish dissident organizations, the Stern Group and the Irgun Zvai Leumi. These were classed, with some justification, by the British as terrorist organizations and, since they were not responsible to the Jewish Agency nor to Hagana, it was vital to have some forewarning of

WANTED

The persons whose names and photographs appear hereunder escaped from detention at Latroun in the night of 31.10.43 and are wanted by the Police under the Emergency Regulations.

Information may be given at any time to any Police Officer or at any Police Station.

Jerusalem 15.11.43

A. SAUNDERS
Inspector General

اعلان

ان الإشخاص الموضحة اسمائهم وصورهم ادناه قد فروا من معتقل اللطرون بليلة ۳۱-۱۰-۱۹٤۳ ومطلوبين للبوليس بموجب قانون الطوارى.

يمكن اعطاء الاخبار عنهم في اي وقت كان لاي ضابط بوليس او مركز بوليس.

ا. ساندرس
المفتش العام

۱۵-۱۱-۱۹٤۳

דרושים למאסר

א. סנדרס
המפקח הכללי

15.11.43

האנשים ששמותיהם ותמונותיהם מופיעים כאן ברחו ממעצרם בלטרון בליל 31.10.43 והמשטרה מחפשת אותם בכדי לעצרם לפי התקנות לשעת חרום. את הידיעה אפשר למסור בכל זמן לכל שוטר או לכל תחנת משטרה.

their activities in order to avoid accidental clashes.

The Hagana force was organized as infantry, since this involved only light weapons which could be easily concealed. Though the force contained men capable of operating artillery, armored vehicles and even aircraft as a result of their wartime training, this was understandably impossible, given the clandestine nature of Hagana at that time. The nearest that Hagana got to this was in the formation of a naval company and in the basic training of a number of pilots in an ostensibly civilian flying club.

The acquisition of weapons was a patchy affair. The ebb and flow of war in North Africa had left huge dumps of munitions, in various conditions from scrap to serviceable, and these were carefully milked. Arab 'dealers' were not averse to turning a profit from their putative enemies and frequently sold weapons acquired either by stealth or as scrap. British soldiers were frequently accommodating, selling serviceable equipment as 'scrap' or even smuggling weapons out of their supply dumps for their friends. The result of all this was a motley collection of weapons of every type and vintage, demanding a wide range of ammunition, which would, in a properly-organized army, have led to a logistical nightmare of supply problems. By late 1947, however, the Hagana had managed to build up a stock of some 8,000 rifles, 3,600 submachine guns, 200 machine guns and about 700 mortars of various types, together with sufficient ammunition to sustain them for three days of battle. It was a remarkable achievement but it left a great deal to be desired in the face of Arab threats of war.

The postwar political scene began to resemble a three-cornered fight which had its roots in an over-hasty pre-war British policy decision. In 1939 the British had invited Jews and Arabs to a conference to work out some sort of a future for Palestine, but the Arabs refused to sit down with the Jews and no progress could be made. In desperation, with the prospect of a major war in front of them and anxious to shelve the Palestine problem so that they could deal with the more pressing question of Germany, Britain published a policy document, which laid down that the Jewish settlements in Palestine were to be frozen at their existing level and an independent Palestinian state was to be formed in which an Arab majority would dominate the government. Once the war was over the British tried to enforce this policy, closing Palestine to further Jewish immigration, while both the Jews and Arabs set about attempting to overturn it, attacking each other and the British with impartial vigor.

During 1947, Arab acts of aggression gained in intensity, with clandestine Arab military strength being constantly reinforced from out-

Building an arsenal British troops launched house-to-house raids in an attempt to capture the illegal Hagana arsenals **(above)**. Many Hagana weapons, in fact, were British Army surplus.

Proposed UN partition:
- International zone
- Jewish state
- Arab state

LEBANON

SYRIA

Nazareth
Haifa
Sea of Galilee

Tel Aviv
Jaffa
Nablus

Jericho
Jerusalem
Bethlehem

Mediterranean Sea

Dead Sea

Beersheba

TRANSJORDAN

Negev Desert

EGYPT

Sinai Desert

Aqaba

Proposed partition With the establishment of the United Nations and the ending of the British mandate, a settlement, based on the partition of Palestine into three zones — international, Jewish and Arab — was proposed. With the plan's failure, armed conflict was inevitable.

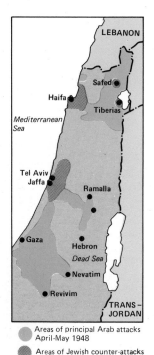

side Palestine. By the end of 1947 it was estimated that there were some 7,000 irregular Arab troops inside the country, plus the regular forces of the Trans-Jordan Arab Legion. Jewish reinforcement, on the other hand, was severely limited by the British blockade, imposed to stem the flood of refugees from the Holocaust. This stopped any worthwhile quantity of men or equipment arriving by sea to strengthen the Hagana. Arab irregulars cut Jewish lines of communication, attacked settlements and murdered individuals, with the ultimate aim of splintering the Jews into small enclaves which could be surrounded and defeated in detail when the time was ripe. Faced with this, Hagana reluctantly decided to abandon its old policy of non-aggression and began to mount large-scale raids and counter-attacks against Arab bases, to blow up frontier bridges and mine roads, so as to reduce the flow of Arab reinforcements into Palestine, and generally try to disrupt the Arab organization.

The British, as reluctant keepers of the peace, inevitably became involved and so Hagana found itself embarked on a guerrilla war on two fronts. To provide the manpower for this, and also prepare for the future, all men of military age were registered and plans were drawn up for the provision of a 25,000-man attack force. Half these men would be war veterans, trained and experienced, about 5,000 would be Palmach members and reservists, and the remainder would be 18- to 25-year old recruits, with the minimum of training. Backing this up would be a defensive force of about 30,000 older men, and a logistic force — supply, transport, engineers and pioneers numbering another 6,000 to 7,000. The only thing that Hagana then possessed, however, was man-

Prelude to war As the British withdrew, the build-up to war between Jew and Arab escalated. The map **(above)** shows the principal areas in which guerrillas of the two sides clashed immediately prior to independence. Armaments need money; the train **(below)** carried the payroll for the staff of Palestine Railways until it was raided by Jewish guerrillas.

Figures in thousands

Survivors Refugees on board the Theodor Herzl dock at Haifa **(above)**, accusing the British of murder. The survivors of the Holocaust **(left)** were determined to reach the sanctuary of Palestine, but the British tried to check the inflow. Of the 600 immigrants landed by this boat **(right)**, all bar 80 were captured and interned in Cyprus. The chart shows the dramatic rise in immigration after Israel opened its doors following independence.

239.4

118.9

27.6

8.4 5.9 3.7

14.5

8.5

17.8 13.1

21.5

1939 1940 1941 1942 1943 1944 1945 1946 1947 1948 1949

The Arabs prepare The Arabs were far superior to the Jews in both manpower and armaments as war drew near, but not in tactics, as events to were to show. General Sir John Glubb — 'Glubb Pasha' — inspects his crack Trans-Jordanian tank crews **(center)**, Trans-Jordanian cavalry parade **(top)** and Arab Legion armored cars set off for the invasion front **(bottom)**. Their mission, according to their king, was 'to quell Zionism'.

Five fronts On paper, the Arab strategy of a concerted attack was sound, but its execution was lacking, due to poor planning and lack of co-ordination **(below)**.

soon as the restraining hand of the British administration was removed. Although at the time the Jews were convinced that the British were actively aiding the Arabs, in hindsight any aid appears to have been more apparent than real; by 1948, all the British were concerned with was keeping both sides apart while they evacuated. They had never particularly wanted the task of governing Palestine, they had shouldered the League of Nations Mandate which had been delegated to them in 1919 unwillingly, and they were now intent upon getting rid of it as gracefully as possible.

While the British made their preparations for departure, the Hagana High Command drew up its final plans to go into effect as soon as the occupation ended. The officially stated aim was 'to gain control of the area allotted to the Jewish State and defend its borders and those of the blocks of Jewish settlement, together with such parts of the Jewish population as were outside those borders, against military or para-military forces operating from bases inside or outside the Jewish State.' In order to implement this plan, it would be necessary to mount operations against advanced Arab camps and bases, to fight for and capture those areas inside the Jewish state which were currently occupied by Arabs, to blockade and besiege Arab areas, so as to bring economic pressure to bear on the enemy, and generally to secure the entire area allocated to the Jews, by force of arms where necessary.

As the date of final British withdrawal (this was to be completed by May 1948) drew closer, the tempo of Arab aggression increased, and finally the Jewish High Command decided to act. In the last week of April three key actions were undertaken. The first was Operation Nahshon, carried out by a force of some 1,500 Hagana, to force open the road to Jerusalem. This had been closed for several weeks by Arab forces, leading to severe hardships for the Jewish population of the city. The only blot on the operation was in its opening states when a force of Irgun irregulars cleared the village of Deir Yassin, and in the confused fighting killed a number of women and children as well as Arab irregulars. This led to a revenge attack by the Arabs who destroyed a Hagana convoy en route to the Jewish University on Mount Scopus outside Jerusalem a few days later.

The next operation was aimed at opening the Haifa road to the Valley of Jezreel. This area had long been used by the Hagana as a training and manoeuver area, so that most of the men and all the commanders were familiar with it. The Arabs were soundly defeated and quantities of weapons and ammunition were captured. Once the road was cleared the Hagana turned to Tel Aviv itself; the British announced that they were

power; it could not clothe all its troops in uniform, it had not worked out any system of pay and allowances, and, apart from the men with previous military service, discipline was relatively poor. The problems of administering a totally irregular force — for there was no legal basis for the conscription of young men, nor was there any sort of national treasury from which to pay them — were enormous, and they were not helped by the somewhat careless attitude to routine administration shown by many unit commanders, who considered that they were there to fight, not to fill in forms and shuffle pieces of paper about.

When the United Nations called for the end of the British presence and the partition of Palestine in November 1947, it became obvious that war was inevitable. Neither the Jews nor the Arabs favored the idea, though the Jews were prepared to try to make it work, given goodwill on the part of the Arabs. The Arabs, on the other hand, were determined to render the plan unworkable and to throw the Jews into the sea by force of arms as

Into battle Israeli forces rush to take up position in their armed jeeps in face of the Arab onslaught **(below)**. Though much of their equipment was makeshift, their will to win brought them success; the Israeli troops **(bottom)** are examining the wreckage of an Egyptian airplane, shot down during a bombing raid on Tel Aviv.

holding only the port area, for their evacuation, and this precipitated a battle for control of the remainder of the city. The Hagana forces had the advantage of the high ground surrounding Tel Aviv and, after a sharp fight, the Arabs were dislodged and the city secured.

The third operation was the clearing of the district between Tel Aviv and Jaffa. Jaffa had been a hotbed of Arab sniping and terrorism, and a force of Irgun irregulars began an offensive against the Arabs in the city to coincide with the approach of the Hagana forces. The Arabs fled and the Jews took over.

These were the opening moves of what has since become known as the War of Independence, the more formal phase of which began on 14 May 1948 with David Ben-Gurion's Declaration of Independence, followed a few hours later by an Egyptian air raid on Tel Aviv. On the following day the infant state of Israel was invaded simultaneously by armies from Egypt, Trans-Jordan, Syria and Lebanon, a total of about 24,000 men with an overwhelming superiority in fire-

Taking control Even before the final British withdrawal, Hagana was flexing its muscle in the cities. Here, Hagana troops man a sandbag barricade during a clash with Arab terrorists in Tel Aviv.

Swearing allegiance With independence on 28 June 1948, the irregular Hagana became the official army of Israel. At this parade in Tel Aviv, Hagana troops take the oath of allegiance to the new state.

was halted; the Egyptians launched an artillery bombardment and then advanced with tanks and armored cars. One tank was stopped by the settlement's solitary bazooka and another set on fire by a home-made Molotov cocktail, while two more were immobilized by a field of extemporised land-mines. After half a day of bitter fighting the Egyptians disengaged, circled around the settlement, and moved forward once more to be finally brought to a halt at Ashdod, some 35km from Tel Aviv, by a broken bridge.

As the column waited in the gathering dusk for engineers to repair the damage, four Israeli Avia fighter-bombers swept out of the sky and deluged the Egyptian forces with machine gun and cannon fire and 500-lb bombs. The shock was enormous; the Arab forces had no idea that the Israelis had such potent aircraft, and, in spite of furious counter-fire put up by the Egyptian troops, the damage done was totally unexpected. Fearful of what further shocks might be in store, the remnants of the column started up, turned round and returned to the safety of their own defensive lines. With this withdrawal, the threat to Tel Aviv evaporated. Little did the Egyptians know that these four aircraft represented the whole of Israel's fighter-bomber force at that time, and that two of them were destroyed as a result of the attack.

The north was invaded by Syrian and Lebanese forces, both of whom were held up by direct attack and by deceptive stratagems of various sorts; one Iraqui armored column was halted by settlers with Molotov cocktails, while another Iraqui force was deceived by the stratagem of driving convoys of Israeli trucks forward throughout the night, with blazing headlights, giving the im-

power. On paper they should have conquered Palestine in a week; they were regular troops, trained, well organized, properly supplied, fully equipped, and they held the initiative. Against this force the Israelis mustered about 18,000 fighting men with 10,000 rifles, 3,600 submachine guns, four elderly French mountain guns smuggled in from Mexico, some bazookas, and two tanks 'which had been 'liberated' from a British depot (with the help of some British soldiers) as far back as 1945.

In fact the tenacity of the Israeli defence shocked the invaders. The Egyptian Army, for instance, rolled across the Sinai Desert without interruption, passed through a number of Arab villages to the plaudits of the occupants, and then came up against an isolated Jewish settlement which had prepared defensive lines. The advance

Independence proclaimed
David Ben Gurion, first premier of Israel, reads the declaration of independence.

pression of a strong force of reinforcements arriving. What the Iraquis did not know was that the trucks were empty and that they drove back without lights in order to make a succession of well-lit return trips.

Having fought the Arabs to a stalemate, the second phase of the war began on 11 July with an Israeli attack — what would later be called a 'pre-emptive strike' — against the Arab Legion. In defiance of the UN observers, both sides had smuggled in reinforcements of both men and weapons during the truce, but the Israelis were far more successful in this, having had more practice at it during the years of their clandestine operations in Palestine. The Israeli Air Force now began to have more influence on the war. Czechoslovakian Avias had begun to arrive in some numbers and were being manned by Jewish veterans of various air forces. The Israeli plan was to hold the Egyptian, Iraqui and Lebanese forces at bay in the south and north respectively, while the main effort went into raising the siege of Jerusalem and defeating the Arab Legion there. The plan was moderately successful, though the Arab Legion survived to fight another day due to a second intervention by the United Nations.

This second cease-fire had no time limit; it was supposed to lead to a permanent settlement by Count Bernadette, the UN mediator, and while negotiations dragged on the Israelis brought in more men and equipment, building up their strength to almost 60,000 men.

In early October the Egyptians began shooting at Israeli convoys which, under the terms of the cease-fire, were permitted to carry food to isolated settlements in the Negev which had been cut off by the Egyptian advance. Taking this as *causus belli*, the Israelis responded with a well-prepared and sudden attack on the Egyptian positions in the south. Beersheba was captured and the Egyptian Army driven from Ashdod and Majdal into the Gaza Strip. After a week of hard fighting the Egyptian front had collapsed, a third of their force had been surrounded, and the Negev had largely been cleared.

A week later the Israeli forces struck in northern Galilee — this time against the Arab Liberation Army, a motley collection of Lebanese troops and guerillas from various Arab countries led by an ex-Syrian army major. Within hours, this force was broken up and ejected from Israel in disorder. There followed a lull until December when, once again, the Israelis fell on the Egyptians and gave them a severe mauling, their complete destruction only being prevented by the Egyptian government hastily agreeing to an armistice. Negotiations began in January, with the Egyptians signing an armistice agreement the following month. In due course the other Arab nations, with the exception of Iraq, followed suit. As

Birth of a nation A parade to mark the opening of new Jerusalem-Tel Aviv road **(above)** is led by two of the jeeps used to break through the Arab lines and raise the siege of Jerusalem during the war of independence. The Israelis were quick to stake out their boundaries; the Israeli flag is planted at Eilat **(right)** as part of Operation Fact .

a final reminder of their ability, and to hasten the laggard signatories, two Israeli brigades advanced through the Negev in March and secured the coastal area around Eilat on the Red Sea.

The War of Independence therefore ended with the Israeli forces in possession of the whole of Galilee, a strip of central Palestine between the coast and Jerusalem, and the Negev. The control of Jerusalem itself was divided between Israel and Trans-Jordan. In total, the area now occupied was slightly larger than that allotted to the Israelis by the original United Nations resolution. The Arab nations, for their part, were in severe disarray; one of the most significant features of the war had been the lack of cooperation between the various Arab invading forces, who seemed perfectly happy to sit and see the army of a fellow Arab nation cut to pieces by the Israelis without lifting a finger to help.

So far as the Israelis were concerned, the War of Independence had demonstrated various fundamental features which were to be capitalized upon in future years. These were tenacious defence; the ability to improvise; the ability to deceive; the superior motivation of men fighting for their homeland; the qualities of self-reliance and initiative, evident down to the lowest ranks; the ability to conceive and execute audacious plans and tactics; and an acute ability to perceive the enemy's weaknesses and exploit them. Moreover the simultaneous ability to fight a war against far superior forces and at the same time bring in men and equipment to build up the military base of the country until it considerably exceeded that of the enemy was proof of the fervor and intensity with which the Israelis were prepared to defend their homeland.

Preserving the peace Even after the War of Independence, security remained strict throughout most of Israel. Israeli police and Hagana **(left)** check Arabs entering the Tel Aviv area.

At the end of the 1948 war the Israeli forces were organized on a somewhat shaky basis, units having been formed as and when men and equipment became available. The following few years were spent in clearing away the deadwood of redundant and obsolete equipment, bringing some sort of order into supply and logistics, and constructing a more formal organization of fighting units. The background to this consolidation, however, was not peaceful. During the early 1950s, border raids by Palestinian and other Arab guerillas became a constant thorn in the Israeli side, and matters came to a head when, in 1955, President Nasser of Egypt announced a military agreement with Soviet Russia for the supply of arms. Israel turned to the USA without success, then to France with the result that the French, searching for a reliable ally to support their interests in the area, agreed to supply the Israelis with modern armored vehicles and aircraft.

Then, in 1956, the Egyptian leader, Colonel Nasser, seized the Suez Canal from the Anglo-French owned Suez Canal Company. In addition, a new alliance between Egypt, Jordan and Syria was announced, which had as its sole aim a combined attack against Israel. Faced with this threat, the Israeli forces decided to act decisively before the new triumvirate became operational, taking the opportunity of the planned Franco-British operation against the Egyptians to regain control of the canal to divert attention from their own preparations. Since it was fairly obvious that the eventual Franco-British attack would be directed against the Canal Zone, and since the Egyptians had withdrawn most of their forces from the

Armed vigilance The Israelis recognized that peace would be precarious, especially on their borders. The Israeli soldier **(left)** is demonstrating the stripping and maintenance of a German MG34 machine gun to settlers at Negba, on the southern Egyptian frontier. An Egyptian border post can be seen through the open door. Volunteers for the army were welcomes; this picture **(below)** shows Arab, Druse and Circassian volunteers lined up for inspection.

The **1956 war** Face with a new foe in Egypt's Colonel Nasser, Israel determined to strike first. An Israeli Sherman leads the way **(right)**, as Israeli infantry advance towards the Suez Canal. Egyptian losses in men and equipment were high **(bottom right)**, since they were fighting a war on two fronts. As the Israelis attacked, an Anglo-French task force was approaching Port Said, its task to regain control of the Suez Canal, which Nasser had nationalized. Two British Centurion tanks patrol a street in Port Said after the invasion **(below)**. US intervention — the US ambassador shakes hands with Colonel Nasser **(right)** — was to lead to cease-fire and withdrawal.

Sinai to protect the Canal, the chances of an Israeli success in that area were good.

Since 1948 the Israeli Army had been reduced to a regular force of some 12,000 men; this could rapidly be fleshed out to over 50,000 by calling out the first reserve — all men who had performed military training as conscripts and had been released back to civilian life. More reservists were also available if needed, and their mobilization would bring the total strength to over 250,000 men. In this instance the first reserve and about 100,000 second reserve were mobilised, bring the army's strength up to about 150,000. These were organized in 16 brigade groups, some of which were classed as armored formations. Others provided frontier defence troops and mobile reserves.

Operation Kadesh, as the Israeli plan was named, began with a move towards Jordan by an airborne brigade, an ostentatious manoeuver which was backed up by a well-advertised curfew on the frontier. This was intended to prevent Arab movement in the frontier area, ostensibly to prevent observation of Israeli troop movements, but, in fact, it was simply a smokescreen to focus atten-

tion on that area while things were happening elsewhere. While this was going on, a strike force had assembled in the Negev in conditions of strict secrecy, and on 29 October it struck across the border, an armored brigade in the vanguard with a parachute battalion dropped ahead, close to the Mitla Pass, a key bottleneck on the invasion route. This advance was two-pronged; one element moved down the Gulf coast towards Sharm-el-Sheikh, while the other, major, force struck across the Sinai desert towards the Gulf of Suez. A third attack was launched across the northern Sinai towards Abu Ageila and the Suez Canal. The whole operation had been carefully planned in phases; at the end of th first phase it would be possible to halt and review the situation. If the Egyptians proved too hard to beat decisively, or if the major powers decided to intervene, then the Israeli forces could be pulled back with little harm done. But if the Egyptians proved to be weak, and if the major nations were preoccupied with their own affairs, then the operation could roll forward. The ultimate objective was to reach the Suez Canal and seize the Gaza Strip.

This is not the place to examine the 1956 war

exhaustively; details will be examined in a later chapter. Here, we are solely concerned with its place in the development of the Israeli armed forces. To summarize, it is enough to say that within a week a third of the Egyptian Army had been soundly beaten, the Egyptian Air Force had been destroyed and Sinai and the Gaza Strip had been secured — all at a cost of no more than 200 Israeli dead and four taken prisoner. 50,000 Egyptians had been captured, while vast quantities of arms and equipment were taken back to Israel, where much of it was refurbished and put into Israeli service.

On the Israeli side the same qualities which had shown up in the 1948 war were still prominent, most of all the propensity to take risks. Indeed, most foreign critics felt that the Israelis had cut things somewhat fine in the risks they took, and, had one or two Egyptian positions held out rather longer, then the end result could well have been different. It is believed that half of the Israeli army's vehicles required major repair after the war was over, and in the light of this after only five days of combat, one suspects a degree of initiative which was close to recklessness. On the other hand, nobody knew their enemy as well as the Israelis did, and they were undoubtedly on sound psychological ground in their assessment of the Egyptian capabilities and weaknesses.

The Arab-Israeli conflict continued with the 1967 'Six-Day War' and the 1973 Yom Kippur wars, but consideration of these can be left until later, since the thesis we have set out to detail had been established by 1960. The Israelis had progressed from operating a guerilla force struggling against guerillas and operating under the shadow of an, at best, neutral governing body, to a regularly constituted, professionally-manned, well-equipped army, navy and air force fighting against guerillas and regulars, interchangeably. From equipping themselves from the dregs of a major war and the scourings of scrap yards around the world, the Israelis were building up a formidable fighting machine, equipped with some of the best weapons from France and Finland, supplemented by a mass of captured modern Soviet equipment. At the same time, Israel was slowly building up its own defence industry to the point that by the 1980s it is fully capable of manufacturing almost any war material it requires from its own resources. In less than 20 years the Israeli armed forces had developed from a clandestine force of irregular infantry to a balanced force of all arms which was capable of taking on and defeating any neighboring army, even though such an army might be larger and, on paper, better equipped. It is an achievement of which any nation could be proud and it is unlikely that any other nation in the world could have accomplished it.

The Machine's Structure

WITH THE POSSIBLE EXCEPTION of Switzerland, it is hard to think of any country in which the armed forces are so well integrated into national life as they are in Israel. In both countries the able-bodied male population are all considered as potential members of the defence forces in the event of national emergency, and in Israel the liability is taken further since the female population are also held to be available for duty. This applied to the whole Jewish and Druse community, but not to the Christians and Moslems, who, however, may volunteer if they wish to do so. Indeed, the Israeli Defence Force is unique in that, so far as the Jewish and Druse people are concerned, it is not possible to walk into a recruiting office and volunteer for regular service; the only method of induction is conscription, though a conscript can decide voluntarily to convert compulsory service into a regular military career.

Men and women both become liable for service at the age of 18. The period of conscription is 36 months for men and 24 months for women, during which basic training is conducted, followed by special-to-arm training. At the end of the compulsory period, and providing no state of emergency obtains, the conscript is released to resume civilian life, but has a continuing reserve liability up to 55 for men and 34 for women. During this period each individual is required to attend

Ready for action An Israeli infantryman poses in full battle kit with his Galil 5.56mm rifle **(left)**, while Israeli infantry are seen on the attack **(below)**. One man covers, the other moving rapidly to take up a firing position. The Israeli armed forces are highly organized **(right)** and it is thanks to this organization that they owe a major part of their efficiency. Army, navy and air force are conscript, Israelis becoming liable for conscription at the age of 18 and staying on the reserve up to the age of 55 for men and 34 for women. The periods of conscript service are 36 and 24 months respectively.

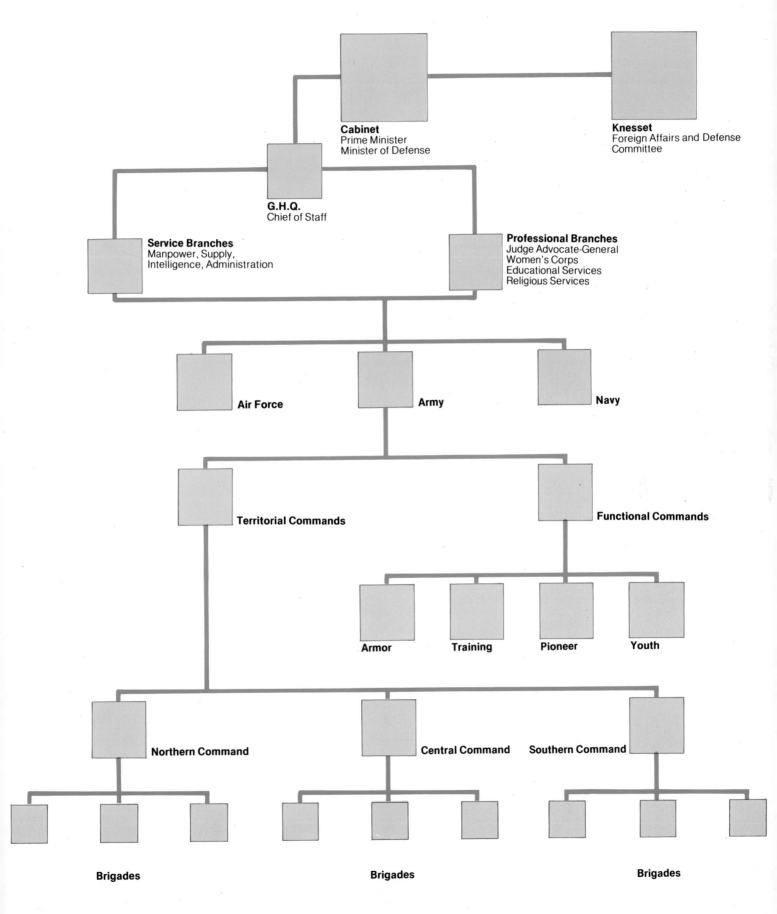

Cabinet
Prime Minister
Minister of Defense

Knesset
Foreign Affairs and Defense
Committee

G.H.Q.
Chief of Staff

Service Branches
Manpower, Supply,
Intelligence, Administration

Professional Branches
Judge Advocate-General
Women's Corps
Educational Services
Religious Services

Air Force

Army

Navy

Territorial Commands

Functional Commands

Armor

Training

Pioneer

Youth

Northern Command

Central Command

Southern Command

Brigades

Brigades

Brigades

Instant readiness
Crewmen hurry to mount their Centurion tanks during a readiness exercise **(below)**, while Centurions exercise in the southern Israeli desert shortly after the Egyptian announcement of the blockade of the Gulf of Akaba in May 1967 **(top)**. Israeli mobilization is highly efficient; within a few hours, the peace-time strength of the defences forces can be increased from approximately 120,000 conscripts and 40,000 regulars to a total strength of around 500,000.

refresher training camps for one month every year in order to be instructed in new weapons and practise in his or her military skills. Both men and women can also be called upon for additional training one day per month, though this is usually consolidated into a three-day period every three months. Upon reaching the age of 39 this annual liability is reduced to fourteen days per year. Officers and NCOs are liable for an additional week of annual training.

The population of Israel is about 3.85 million. This produces two annual conscript intakes of about 25,000 each. About 80% of potential male recruits and 60% of potential female ones are actually inducted; the three-year term of service for men means, therefore, that something in the order of 130,000 conscripts are serving at any given moment in peacetime. These are cemented together, trained and led by a regular cadre of about 40,000 professional soldiers, sailors and airmen, and it is this regular force which keeps the IDF in operation on a day-to-day peacetime basis.

The threat of war brings into action Israel's super-efficient mobilization machinery. This has been honed to such a degree of perfection that the IDF can be expanded from its peacetime strength to about 500,000 within an amazing 72 hours. Every reservist knows precisely what his or her task upon mobilization is, what unit to join and where he or she is to report. All he or she requires is the order to put these instructions into effect. For this purpose every unit and sub-unit is given a code-name; when mobilization is ordered, the military staffs merely issue a list of code-names to the radio network which broadcasts them nationwide. *Sons of Zion, Eidelweiss, Winter Rose, Motor Car, George Washington* — every phrase has a specific meaning, and as the reservists hear the code-name of their unit, so they pick up their haversacks, make their farewells to friends and family, and go to the appointed rendezvous, where transport awaits to take them to their post of duty. The code-words are changed periodically. The system not only provides the fastest method of disseminating the call to arms; it also does not compromise security by directly identifying the different units, so that alien listeners do not know whether an armored division, say, or a field sanitary unit is being brought up to strength.

The issuing of the orders for mobilization is the bottom rung of a ladder which has its topmost rung in the highest political level — the Prime Minister's cabinet. Within the cabinet is the Minister of Defense, and parallel with the cabinet is the Foreign Affairs and Defense Committee of the Knesset, the legislative assembly of the State of Israel. The broad outlines of national defence policy are decided between the Knesset and cabinet and it is then the responsibility of the Minister of Defense to pass on this policy to the headquarters of the Israeli Defence Force.

The GHQ IDF contains the General Staff, headed by the Chief of Staff who is also Commander of the Armed Forces. The staff is split up in the usual manner of such organizations in any army; there is a coordinating HQ, separate branches dealing with Supply, Plans, Intelligence and Personnel, and an administrative echelon responsible for communications and the day-to-day running of the staff as a military unit.

Once the government's policy is passed down to the General Staff, it is their responsibility to implement it. They decide upon operational contingency plans which will allow the IDF to function in accordance with the policy; they decide upon the strength and composition of forces which will permit those plans to be carried out efficiently — how many tanks an armored division should have and what type they should be, how many men in an infantry division, what percentage of the force should be paratroopers, commandos, skilled mechanics or nurses, and how many transport aircraft the Chel Ha'Avir (the Israeli Air Force) require to move how many troops how far, for instance. They must consider the amount, type and degree of training required by the various elements of the IDF, and whether special training might be needed to fit particular units for particular tasks in the event of a specific war plan being put into action. They must consider what neighboring countries are doing, what armament they have or are about to acquire, what their potential is, and how any possible action would interact with the national policy, leading to a consideration of what plans are needed to counter various likely moves on Israel's borders. As all of these factors are broadly considered, discussed and decided, so the administrative sections of the staff structure take them and reduce them to detailed orders and instructions which they then disseminate throughout the IDF.

The Chief of Staff has a Deputy Chief and is assisted in his deliberations by the heads of the four staff branches and by the chiefs of the services — Armor, Infantry, Artillery, Air, Naval, Supply, Ordnance, Women's Services, and also the heads of the Medical, Legal, Religious and Education services. These act as the professional advisors to the Chief of Staff, providing him with detailed information on the state of the various branches of the service, morale, health and on every conceivable factor which might affect military decisions.

Beneath the General Staff lie the forces in the field. For administrative purposes Israel is divided into three territorial commands. — Northern, Central and Southern. These more or less corres-

Basic training Israeli training is tough and realistic in all branches of the defence forces. Recruits **(top)** are learning how to set up a bivouac in the field; armed infantry **(above)** move forward in column, ready for any confrontation with opposing forces.

ment, and also for the basic training of armor personnel before they are sent to individual units. Training Command is responsible for the overall quality of training, for the evaluation of training methods and for the economic utilization of training facilities throughout the country. It also controls the allocation of the costly modern simulation devices. Pioneer Command is responsible for coordinating military and agricultural activities in the so-called security settlements on the Israeli border, while Youth Command administers the pre-military training of 14-18 year old youths in preparation for their conscription.

Higher level training for senior officers to fit them for command posts, is carried out by the National Defense College, a tri-service establishment which conducts courses in strategic planning and in military-political affairs. There is also the Command and General Staff College, which concentrates upon the more practical aspects of General Staff operations, such as tactical, planning, logistics, intelligence and similar subjects. In addition, officers are frequently sent on attachment to staff and war colleges in other countries.

The largest combat unit within the army is the brigade. There are three types — Infantry, Armor and Airborne. Should the demands of a particular operation require a larger formation than this to be wielded as one, then a Brigade Group HQ is formed, which controls one or more brigades. In effect, this resembles a division in any other army, but, in contrast, it is not immutable. The HQ is assembled as and when required and the formations placed under it can be any combination which appears to be suited to the task at hand. As soon as this is completed, then the Group HQ is disbanded and the individual formations revert to their previous status.

Although the air force is under the orders of the General Staff and its own staff is integrated within the General Staff structure, it enjoys a fair degree of independence. Its basic formation is the squadron, individual squadron establishments being determined by the type of aircraft employed and the tactical function to be performed, whether this is ground attack, interception, transport, liaison or whatever. The deployment of the air force against enemy air forces is entirely in the hands of the Air Staff, but its employment in conjunction with the ground forces is carefully coordinated through the General Staff with the army units concerned.

In a similar manner the Navy Staff is integrated with the General Staff but enjoys autonomy in its own element. So far as naval operations against enemy ships are concerned, the naval staff are free to determine their own priorities and plans, but where cooperation with other services is required, then the General Staff structure again acts as the coordinating agency.

pond to the chief danger spots; the Northern Command faces towards Lebanon and Syria, the Central Command Jordan and the Southern Command Egypt. The three are the administrative and operational skeleton of the defence structure; they have full responsibility for administering and supplying the units within their region, and they are also responsible for mobilization and training, subject to the overall policy decisions of GHQ. It is the task of the commands to deploy troops on the ground in accordance with the General Staff's plans, but it is the General Staff's responsibility to say what troops go into which command; this means that the individual commands must be considerably flexible in their organization, since their tasks can vary from one week to another as units are moved into or out of their sphere of responsibility in accordance with the overall plans for national defence.

Superimposed over the geographical commands are the functional commands — Armor, Training, Pioneer and Youth — which are responsible for the standards of training throughout the army within their respective spheres. The Armor Command is responsible for deciding types of armored vehicle and arma-

In the desert Israeli soldiers are thoroughly acclimatized to desert conditions. An infantry squad is briefed for action **(above)**; the crew of a 120mm self-propelled mortar man their machine gun to practise local defence **(left)**.

The Women's Corps was, for many years, unique because it was totally integrated with the remainder of the IDF; though this is now the case with other women's forces, notably in the USA, it is doubtful if any other women's force enjoys such a total degree of assimilation. In its early days the force was organized on separate lines, very similar to the way in which servicewomen were organized in the British and US armies during the Second World War; it was completely independent, with its own headquarters, staff and formations. Recruitment was distinct from the rest of the IDF, control was entirely in female hands, and the members of the force lived in separate camps.

This system was found not to meet either the needs of the IDF or suit the structure of Israeli society, so it was changed to make the Women's Corps an integral part of the armed services.

Contrary to popular belief, however, Israeli women are not trained as combat troops, though they are naturally instructed in the use of arms for purposes of self-defence. The reason for this is entirely because of the potential enemy, since the Arabs have made it clear, more than once, that they regard Israeli women soldiers as being no different to their male counterparts and would be unlikely to accord them any special treatment during war.

Total war Women and men have equally important roles to play in Israel's defence forces. Members of the Women's Army Corps march from Hulda to Jerusalem during the annual four-day competitive march **(below)**. An Israeli girl signaller, wearing as little as possible to combat the desert heat, passes on information on Arab shipping movements in the Strait of Tiran during the 1967 campaign **(right)** and three women tank instructors brief male recruits on basic operation procedures **(far right)**.

The Israeli Navy

FOR MUCH OF ITS HISTORY, the principal task of the Israeli Navy has been that of coastal defence and preserving the territorial integrity of Israel. The traditional naval role, adopted by the major sea powers, of keeping the sea-lanes open, or, in other words, ensuring the safe passage of supply ships to and from their country in time of war, did not figure largely in Israeli naval thinking for the excellent reason that the whole basis of Israeli defence planning lay in speed of execution. In such a case, with the course of a war determined in a matter of days, there is little or no chance to replenish the national stockpile by shipping in armaments, stores or food; such supplies as are needed are so desperately required that only air transport will suffice. Thus, the long and leisurely business of chartering ships, loading them, sailing them and finally unloading them has no place in the Israeli scheme of warfare and there was little need for the naval forces to adopt the traditional role mentioned above.

In its early days, the Israeli Navy was more or less based upon traditional British ideas, probably due to the number of its sailors who had served with the Royal Navy during the war. This led to tactical and strategic consideration of the traditional naval roles — convoy duty, submarine and anti-submarine warfare, and, of course, keeping the sea-lanes open. But the actual performance of these tasks, had they been required, would have been severely hampered by the equipment available. Due to the highly specialized nature of traditional warships, and the difficulties encountered in trying to obtain them, Israel's early naval force was composed of a heterogenous collection of craft culled from all over the world, chosen simply for their availability and not for their fitness to fill any planned roles. Destroyers, frigates, submarines and motor torpedo boats were bought here and there, with the one common factor of ob-

Mistress of the seas A Saar class Fast Attack Craft on patrol, with 40mm gun in the forward turret. The launcher units for the craft's deadly Gabriel missiles can be seen abaft the bridge structure. Displacing 250 tons when full loaded, the class can achieve the formidable speed of over 40 knots.

solescence as political and economic restraints prevented the acquisition of modern vessels. In addition the strategic position of Israel, and the immediate threats to its territorial integrity, were such that the lion's share of what money was available went to the army and air services, since it was thought rightly that their equipping and strengthening was more vital to Israel's survival than the provision of modern warships.

These attitudes fitted together very nicely. Since there was little money available, it was just as well that the navy had no major ambition; since the available ships could be used for more or less any role, then any and every role appeared acceptable. But gradually the prevalent theory of a short war pushed the naval force into the coastal defence role, and, although its sailors might have had other ideas, matters remained like this for several years.

The short war theory appeared to be borne out

by the events of the Sinai campaign in 1956 and by the Six Day War of 1967. The war of attrition which followed the latter event dented the theory to some extent, however. It was found that munition consumption could outstrip Israel's ability to re-supply its forces, and, while air-freighting could be countenanced in emergencies, it was not suitable or economic to rely on it for any length of time. The now-leaking theory was holed further by the Yom Kippur War of 1973. Though this lasted barely three weeks, the Israelis found themselves running extremely short of supplies of some types of equipment by the end of it.

By this time, though, the navy had begun to re-think its role in any case. One of the most fundamental reasons for this was a dramatic incident in 1967, when a surface-to-surface shipborne missile was used in combat for the first time in military history. In it, ships of the Egyptian Navy were being blockaded in Port Said by an Israeli flotilla. An Egyptian patrol boat, anchored in the harbor, fired a Soviet-manufactured Styx SSN-2 missile which struck and sank the Israeli destroyer Eilat which was part of the blockading force. The incident, in which a heavily armed conventional warship was sent to the bottom of the Mediterranean by a lightweight patrol boat without the latter even bothering to cast off and leave harbor, set the navies of the world on their heels and led to some unprecedented strategic and tactical re-thinking. No Western navy had, at that time, any weapon resembling the Soviet Styx, and its potentialities came as a thunderclap.

Naturally enough, the Israelis were also impressed by the success of the missile attack and began to take stock of the naval situation as it af-

fected them and their area of operations. The Egyptian navy was equipped with a number of fast Styx-armed patrol boats, and, after the demonstration of their capabilities, there was no doubt that they presented a considerable danger. The Israeli Navy's existing ships — four old destroyers, two old submarines, an ex-German coast-guard cutter, three old American landing craft and a dozen motor torpedo boats dating from the 1930s — were no sort of counter to modern ships and weapons, since they were not just inadequate in numbers, but also lacked any sort of armament which could cope with the Egyptians.

Already, in the early 1960s, the Israeli defence establishment had begun to re-assess the navy's role and had begun to plan for a small, but modern, force of fast attack craft armed with suitable missiles. The Gabriel missile, which was eventually selected, was already in its early stages of development, though at that time it was an orphan project looking for a sponsor. Once the navy had defined its new role, Gabriel found itself a father and the project took on a new sense of urgency, to be accelerated further when the Styx incident proved the validity of ship-launched missiles. A further incentive was the appreciation that a modern vessel, with up-to-date armament, could achieve the same results with a crew of 40 officers and men as could a destroyer with a crew of over 200, since, in the final analysis, the latter could do no more damage than the new ship. The new philosophy was summed up in the statement made by an Israeli Navy Doctrine paper: 'We must not wait to intercept the enemy off our own coast, but go to meet him and seek him out wherever he may be, thereby depriving him of the initiative. This is the best starting-

Into action Corvettes of the Israeli Navy guard the bay of Tel Aviv against possible air attack by Egyptian airplanes in October 1948. At the time, this was almost the entire Israeli naval strength.

point for the defence of our own coastline and keeps the potential threat in enemy waters.'

The keystone to the re-organization of the Israeli Navy was the realization that, at that time, there was no sure method of defence against the Styx or, indeed, any other similar missile. Therefore the best defence was attack with a similar missile system against which, by definition, there could be no effective defence. Development of the Israeli Gabriel went ahead at full pace, and a suitable fast attack craft was devised to carry it. The first setback came when it was realised that Gabriel would have a maximum operational range of some 18km, about half that of Styx; this is scarcely surprising, since Gabriel is about one-fifth the weight of Styx, but nevertheless it threatened to put the Israelis at a considerable disadvantage. There was, at that time, no prospect of improving Gabriel's performance, so the navy had to sit down and develop a system of tactics which would reduce the imbalance. These included basic considerations of the type of boat, the size and composition of a combat flotilla, and how best to utilize deception tactics and the technology of electronic warfare to confuse an enemy. As far as the last of these is concerned, the longer range of Styx actually works to its firer's disadvantage, since its increased flight time gives its target more opportunity to decoy it.

By 1973 the Israeli Navy had made considerable progress in its re-equipment, and a good deal of progress in working out a tactical method; the Yom Kippur war gave the opportunity to try out both equipment and theory. By then the force had 14 fast attack craft: two Reshef class, armed with two 76mm guns and six Gabriel missiles; six Sa'ar III class, armed with a single 40mm gun and

The 1967 campaign An Israeli patrol boat, armed with 20mm cannon and heavy machine guns, patrols the Gulf of Akaba in 1967 (left). In this war, the Israeli Navy came face to face with a new threat; the destroyer Eilat (bottom) was sunk on 21 October by a Styx missile fired by an Egyptian patrol boat. The Eilat was the first ship in maritime history to be sunk by a ship-to-ship missile. A Styx is fired (below).

five Gabriels; and three Sa'ar I class, armed with three 40mm guns. One of the Sa'ar I boats was undergoing periodic overhaul and was therefore not available for active service.

The naval command's assessment of the situation on the outbreak of war on 6 October assumed that the Egyptian naval forces would attempt to enforce a blockade of Israel by attacking ships at sea and by bombardment of land targets and shipping close to Israeli harbours. To counter this, it was ordered that 'offensive thrusts (will) be launched to find and destroy enemy vessels and naval forces along the Syrian and Lebanese coasts to the north and around Port Said to the south...' In accordance with this directive, a five-ship combat group left Haifa in the afternoon of 6 October to conduct an offensive sweep to the north. Later that night, some distance southwest of Latakia, the flotilla surprised a Syrian patrol boat, presumably acting as a radar picket, and sank it with gunfire. Shortly afterwards a target was detected close to the Syrian coast. The flotilla turned towards this, which proved to be a minesweeper, but, shortly afterwards, detected a salvo of six Styx missiles approaching it from the south-east. The ship which launched these missiles had not been detected, but now the tactical training adopted by the Israelis began to prove its worth; by a combination of agile manoeuvering and the use of electronic countermeasures the missile salvo was evaded. The flotilla then resumed its approach to the Syrian minesweeper. Once within range, the northernmost Israeli boat fired a series of Gabriel missiles which struck the minesweeper, set it on fire and wrecked it.

The flotilla now turned south to deal with the craft which had fired the Styx missiles, and very soon detected another salvo approaching. Once again a combination of skilfull maneouver and countermeasures enabled the Israelis to evade the attack; one Styx was actually shot out of the air by gunfire. After thus managing to get underneath the enemy's guard, as it were, the Israeli flotilla began launching its own missiles against the Syrian vessels, which proved to be Komar class fast patrol boats. Two of these were destroyed instantly, the third was apparently damaged and made a run for the coast with the intention of beaching, but one of the Israeli boats pursued it and finished it off with gunfire, thus disposing of all the enemy vessels.

On 8 October, with heavy land fighting in progress on the Golan Heights and in the Sinai peninsula, it was thought likely that Egyptian naval forces might try some form of attack against the Israel coastline as a diversionary measure. Accordingly, a second flotilla of fast attack craft left Haifa to undertake an offensive sweep along the Egyptian coast, with orders to pay special attention to the Nile Delta and its vicinity. The flotilla

Gabriel in action A Gabriel missile being launched from a patrol boat **(right)** and the missile in its launcher container on the rear deck **(inset)**. The Gabriel was developed by Israeli Aircraft Industries, starting in 1966. It is one of the most effective ship-to-ship missiles of its type in the world, attacking at wave height and carrying a deadly punch of 150kg of high explosive.

Reshefs in action A flotilla of fast patrol boats sweeps through the Straits of Tiran, a few days after the end of the 1967 war. The crew in the foreground are manning a 20mm oerlikon cannon **(above)**. Two Reshef class fast attack craft **(right)** lie off the Lebanese town of Tyre in support of Israeli ground forces. To obtain these craft, the Israelis launched a daring 'cutting out' operation, sailing them from Cherbourg in the teeth of a French arms embargo, as the press recorded **(bottom right)**.

consisted of six vessels, split into three well-separated pairs.

After some hours of patrolling, and close to midnight, the Israelis detected the approach of an Egyptian formation, consisting of four fast attack craft of the Osa class. As the range closed to 48km the Egyptians launched a salvo of Styx missiles. The Israeli flotilla opened out its formation to provide a multiplicity of targets and thus baffle the oncoming missiles, whilst also embarking on various evasive maneouvers and employing electronic countermeasures. Having thus outwitted the salvo, the Israelis were confronted with another, followed by a third and a fourth, all of which they were able to avoid. By this time the two flotillas were some 30km apart and the Egyptian vessels now turned about and began to run for safety, pursued by the Israelis, who began to gain on them. Once the range was within Gabriel firing distance, the Israeli boats opened fire with successive missiles, each pair of boats engaging a specific Egyptian target.

Within minutes, two Egyptian boats had been blown out of the water and a third was so badly damaged that it limped southwards to beach on the coast, where it was destroyed by gunfire from two of the Israeli boats. The fourth Osa managed to evade the pursuit and escaped. The unscathed Israeli flotilla then turned north and returned to its base.

Small-scale though they were, these two sea battles were of seminal importance, since they

were the first to take place between missile-armed high-speed naval forces. Their result completely vindicated Israeli tactical concepts and their choice of equipment. The problem of encountering a long-range weapon with one of shorter range is not totally novel; the Royal Navy, for instance, had met it over 150 years before when, armed with the short-ranging Carronade cannon, they had encountered the US Navy, with its long-ranging Columbiad cannons, in the War of 1812. Better seamanship occasionally saved the day for the British, allowing them to move in close and batter their opponents into submission, but frequently the Americans were able to stay out of range and bombard the British at their leisure. The long-term answer was to develop equally long-ranging weapons so as to restore the balance. Israel eventually followed this path as well, developing improved models of Gabriel, with a range of almost 40km, as far as the Styx.

In 1973, however, the immediate answer had to lie in superior tactics, and it was these which gave the Israelis victory in their two encounters. The precise nature of the maneouvers that were used have never been divulged, nor have the specific countermeasures that were taken, though it is known that these were a mixture, involving electronic jamming and more direct methods, including close-in gunfire. These, coupled with the greater power and speed of the Israeli vessels, gave them the decisive edge in the battle and enabled them to move inside the range of Styx and outmaneouver the missiles until they were able to launch their own. By that time the Egyptian craft were stern-on, retreating at high speed, and it says much for the guidance system of Gabriel that it was successful against such small and elusive targets. It has been said that this contingency was foreseen by the missile's designers, who went to considerable trouble to devise a guidance system which would cope with exactly this type of target.

The Commander-in-Chief of the Israeli Navy at the present time is Rear-Admiral Michael Barkai; at the time of the 1973 war he was a captain, commanding the guided missile attack force, and was the actual flotilla commander in both the battles described here. The current strength of the Israeli fleet is as follows.

Three patrol submarines
Gal, Tanin and Rahav were built by Vickers of England, (their Type 206) and are 146.7m long, displacing 420 tons when surfaced and 600 tons when submerged. Propelled by the traditional diesel-electric combination, they have a surface speed of 11 knots and 17 knots submerged and are armed with eight 21-in torpedo tubes in the bows. An antiaircraft missile launcher known as SLAM (Submarine-Launched Air-to-air Missile) is carried in the fin, which fires the Blowpipe missile.

Two corvettes

These are as yet un-named and are under construction by Israeli Shipyards Ltd at Haifa; it is possible that a total of six will eventually be built. The corvettes have a displacement of 850 tons, mount four Gabriel II launchers, may have mounts for the American Harpoon missile, and will have two 76mm OTO-Melara guns and six 35mm anti-aircraft guns (probably Oerlikon). Propulsion will be by a combination of diesel and gas turbines, resulting in a maximum speed in excess of 40 knots. The corvettes will each carry a helicopter and will also be armed with a Bofors 375mm anti-submarine rocket launcher.

Twelve Fast Attack Craft (Missile)

This is the Reshef class, of which the first two (Reshef and Keshet) were launched in 1973 and took part in the sea war in that year. Romah and Kidon were launched in 1974. Tarshish and Yobbo in 1975. Six more were ordered in 1975, but this contract was delayed while the yard built a number for export to South Africa. Delivery of the second batch began in 1980; since then a further six have been ordered to bring the eventual total to 18.

The decision to design and build these boats in Israel was taken after problems with overseas sources of supply, particularly after France embargoed the export of 50 Mirage fighter aircraft and the last five Sa'ar class patrol boats the Israelis had ordered. This last problem led to the Cherbourg 'operation' in December 1969, when Israeli

Submarine missile Israel's
three patrol submarines
carry the added punch of
the Slam anti-aircraft missile
launcher in their fins. This
fires the British Blowpipe
missile.

reach a maximum speed of 36 knots.

Twelve Fast Attack Craft (Missile)

The Sa'ar class was commissioned in 1968 and
1969 and built in France to a German design for
political reasons. The vessels were built in two
batches of six, the first batch being armed with
three 40mm guns and sonar, the second with a
single 76mm gun and no sonar. After delivery to
Israel, all twelve were fitted with Gabriel missiles, though the fitting scale is by no means standard and not all the ships have similar armament.
The first batch also had four torpedo tubes, but
these were later dismounted when the Gabriels
were installed.

The 'Sa'ar' class displace 250 tons when fully
loaded, are some 50m shorter than the Reshef,
and can achieve more than 40 knots.

35 Coastal Patrol Craft

The Dabur class are 65m long and displace 35 tons
when fully laden. They are capable of 25 knots
and are armed with two 20mm Oerlikon guns
and two .50 Browning machine guns. The first 12
of these boats were built in the USA, with the remainder being built in Israel. They have
aluminum hulls and have good sea-keeping
qualities in rough weather. They are deployed in
both the Mediterranean and Red Seas. A special
design feature is the fact that they can be easily
lifted out of the water and moved rapidly across
country on special transporter-trailers. The armament specified above is standard, but different
vessels have other variations; some of this class
are thought to carry an unspecified short-range
missile, for instance, but this has not been confirmed officially by the Israelis.

Two Fast Attack Craft (Missile)

The Dvora class is a private venture by Israeli
Shipyards and is basically an improved Dabur
class. The displacement has been increased to 47
tons, the length to 75m, and the speed to 36 knots.
Armament is thought to be two Gabriel launchers and two single 20mm cannon. The Dvora is
the smallest missile craft the Israelis have
developed to date; if it proves successful after its
trials with the Israeli Navy, it is likely more will
be taken into service.

Two Coastal Patrol Craft

These craft have no class name, being ex-United
States Coastguard boats, with glass-fiber-
reinforced plastic hulls, two diesel engines driving hydrojets to give 25 knots, and armament of
two .50 Browning machine guns. It is unlikely
that the Israelis will take up the design.

Two Hydrofoils

These are known provisionally as the Flagstaff 2
class and are being built in the USA; according to
reports, ten more will be built in Israel under
license if the first two prove successful. The
original Flagstaff was built for the US Navy by the
Grumman Aircraft Corporation and is currently

crews succeeded in sailing the impounded boats
out of Cherbourg harbour and home to Haifa.

The incident showed that the Israeli Navy
possessed the same spirit of initiative and devil-
may-care attitude as the army and air force.
When the embargo fell, Israeli sailors were
already manning the boats, so that trials could be
completed before the delivery was formally accepted as satisfactory. Somehow, the Israelis acquired sufficient fuel, food and water — plus
other essentials — and on Christmas Eve 1969
they simply shipped anchor and sailed for Israel.
It says much for the design of the class that the
boats coped with the Bay of Biscay in winter.

In general arrangement the Reshef class is a
logical development of the earlier Sa'ar class,
though they have almost twice the firepower and
three times the range of the latter. A further major difference was the incorporation of highly advanced radar and electronic systems which had
been developed entirely in Israel. The Reshefs
were designed specifically for long periods at sea,
carrying a crew of 45 in a high degree of comfort
so that the sailors can operate at peak efficiency
over long period and in high temperatures.

Each vessel carries six Gabriel and four Harpoon missile launchers; the Gabriels are a mixture of Types I and II but the entire fleet will eventually standardise upon the latter. Each ship also
has two 76mm guns and two 20mm Oerlikon cannon. Displacing 415 tons and propelled by four
diesel engines, they can reach 32 knots, though it
is probable that the second and third batches will
have a slightly greater overall length and may

used as a US Coastguard patrol vessel. It uses the conventional arrangement of hydrofoils, in which the forward foil takes some 70 per cent of the weight and the rear foil the remaining 30 per cent. Propelled by a Rolls-Royce gas turbine engine, the craft can reach speeds of well over 40 knots. In US service, Flagstaff has been largely used as a trials and evaluation vessel, carrying various combinations of armament and other technical equipment from time to time; in coastguard service it is armed with an 81mm mortar and two heavy machine guns. The armament the Israelis have selected is still secret, but it is likely to include at least one Gabriel mounting.

These vessels form the backbone of the modern Israeli navy. In addition there are three ex-American landing ships, displacing 1100 tons, for amphibious operations; three 20-ton LCMs (for landing vehicles); three 400-ton and three 180-ton LCTs (for landing tanks), built by Israeli Shipyards. Other ships commissioned into the Israeli Navy include the Ma'oz, an oil-rig tender converted into a Light Forces Support Ship; the Bat Yam and Bat Sheva transports; and one training craft and four Kedma class coastal patrol boats, used by the coastguard and police forces.

The Gabriel missile is the chief form of armament. As we have seen, it was developed by Israeli Aircraft Industries from 1966 onwards and thoroughly proved its operational worth in the 1973 war, when it is credited with sinking a total of nine Egyptian and Syrian warships and severely damaging several more. The Mark I version is 3.35m long and 325mm in diameter; the Mark II version is the same length, but has an increased diameter of 25mm. The wingspan is 1.385m. The missile is launched by a solid-fuel boost rocket, after which a slow-burning sustainer rocket takes over to give a cruise speed of approximately Mach 0.7. The Mark II version uses a more powerful sustainer motor, thus increasing the maximum operational range from about 18km to around 36km. Once the launch ship has located its target by radar or optical sighting, the launcher is aligned accordingly and the missile fired. The initial boost carries it to a height of 75m, after which it moves down to 10m above the waves, its height and course being stabilised by a radio altimeter and a twin-gyroscope inertial platform. Radio commands can be used to control the missile's course directly during the initial part of the flight, after which the semi-active radar fitted in the missile takes over the homing function. The missile can also be programmed to home automatically on to any point source of electronic jamming, so that attempts to jam the homing radar are self-defeating. There are also a number of other electronic options, designed to defeat most types of counter-measure.

In the final phase of its attack the missile sinks as close to the wave-tops as possible, the precise

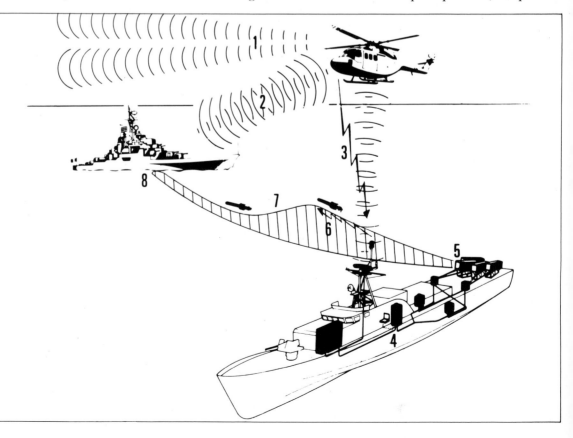

How Gabriel works Gabriel operates in the same way as other ship-to-ship missiles. Optical or radar search (1) locates the target (2) and feeds firing data to the missile ship (3). The ship's computer calculates the firing data (4), selects the missile to be fired and starts the firing sequence. The missile is lauched (5) and, in flight, has fresh information passed to it (6), updating the target's location. The missile responds, steering towards the new location (7) and finally sweeps down to sea level for the final homing stage (8), relying on its internal guidance systems.

height being governed by mechanisms which respond to the state of the sea. This means that the radar 'signature' of the missile tends to be masked by sea clutter, making it extremely difficult to detect and counter. It is thought that one version of the missile is also fitted with a television camera in its nose, which allows the launch operator to select his target if several are on offer and to control the missile directly until impact. The 150kg warhead has a delayed-action fuze to enable it to penetrate the ship's hull or superstructure before detonating.

In addition to building Gabriels for its own navy, Israel has also exported the missile to several countries. These include Argentina, Singapore, Thailand, South Africa and Malaysia, amongst others.

The Harpoon missile is an American design, having been developed by MacDonnell Douglas for the US Navy. There are three versions — for air, surface or submarine launching respectively –the Israelis having chosen the RGM-84A surface version. They ordered 100 in the latter 1970s. Harpoon uses a rocket boost to get airborne, after which a turbojet sustainer takes over to cruise the weapon at Mach 0.9.

The method of operation is similar to that of Gabriel. After a target being detected by radar and the missile aligned, the missile is then programmed with the target's range and location and launched. It has an active radar seeker in its head which seeks for, detects, and locks on to the target when it finds it in the designated 'window' area. The missile then flies very close to the sea, controlled by the conventional radio altimeter. During the final phase of its attack, it can be pre-programmed to either hug the waves as a 'sea-skimmer' or suddenly pull sharply up and then dive down on to the target, the object in the latter case being to inflict as much damage as possible on the relatively vulnerable upperworks and sensor arrays of the target ship. The 230kg warhead is provided with a piercing nose which permits penetration of the ship before the delayed action fuze functions; alternatively, the warhead can be filled with a proximity fuze, which can be programmed to operate at optimum target separation, giving the maximum blast effect against the target's decks, radar antenna, optical devices and other sensors.

According to some reports, certain Israeli ships are now fitted with the French Exocet surface-skimming missile. This operates in much the same way as Harpoon or Gabriel, but there has been no official confirmation that Exocet is actually in Israeli naval service.

Giving support In common with the Israeli Air Force, the Israeli Navy is prepared to support land forces whenever required. Here, seen from the open bow doors of a Landing Ship, Army M113 personnel carriers storm ashore on a Lebanese beach.

The Israeli Air Force

GIVEN THE SUPPORT of the population, building-up an army from scratch is a relatively easy affair; basic weapons — rifles, submachine guns, grenades — are acquired, the keen citizen is given some elementary training, and then sent off to war. Where the enemy is relatively unsophisticated, such a force stands a good chance of surviving and even of winning.

Building an air force along the same lines, however, is a far more daunting task. In the first place, the weapons — aircraft — are far from simple, are difficult to acquire, hard to smuggle, practically impossible to manufacture without a suitable industrial base, expensive and difficult to maintain. In the second place, air force personnel need to be highly skilled, whether they are actually flying the aircraft or, equally vitally, repairing and maintaining them on the ground. No matter how keen or patriotic the citizen is, without expensive and time-consuming training he is useless to an air force. These, plus several other difficulties confronted the infant Israeli Defence Force as it came close to its Independence Day birth. The saga of how the problems were overcome is a fascinating story of determination and endeavour.

The Sherut Avir (Aviation Service) of Hagana had existed in clandestine guise under British rule under the aegis of various civil flying clubs. Two of these, the Carmel Club and the Flying Camel Club had been set up in the early 1930s, and, with age, had gained a respectable image. A third, the Civilian Flying Club, was a late-comer on the scene and was almost entirely a clandestine reconnaisance unit of the Sherut Avir. The clubs were aided by two other organizations — firstly the Aviron Company and secondly the Palestine Air Service. The first bought and sold aircraft and trained pilots quite legitimately, but also acted as an undercover procurement agency for Sherut Avir; the second was a small commercial carrier, which trained far more pilots and ground staff than its civil activities really warranted.

In 1947 therefore the Sherut Avir was able to put a variety of aircraft into the air for military purposes, though they all, without exception, were unsuitable for this role. The Civilian Flying Club contributed a handful of Taylorcraft and ex-Polish light aircraft, most of which were feeling their age, and also managed to legally import two De Haviland DH82A biplanes from Canada and a third from England. More Taylorcrafts were acquired from private owners and from the Aviron Company, which produced a De Haviland Dragon Rapide cabin biplane, while a private donor gave a Seabee amphibian and the Hagana contributed a Fairchild Argus they had captured from an Egyptian smuggler they caught in the Negev. The most unexpected haul came when the British authorities advertised 24 Auster Air Observation

Somewhere in Israel An Israeli F-4E Phantom approaches its airfield for refuelling and rearming in early morning October 1973. The efficiency of Israeli ground crews is such that the turnround between missions is a matter of minutes.

The paras Israeli paratroopers check their equipment before a training flight in 1957. They are following the US practice of using a reserve parachute as well as the static-line type.

Post machines for disposal as scrap; a representative of Aviron hot-footed it to the depot, paid the derisory sum that was being asked for scrap value, and had the aircraft removed immediately. Perhaps stirred from torpor by this rapid response, the British belatedly realized that it might be possible to make something of the 'scrap' and tried to rescind the sale, but it was too late. The Austers vanished from sight, to be stripped and rebuilt, using components of several planes to produce a single serviceable machine, a process known in military circles as 'cannabalizing'. By this means the 24 Austers yielded exactly half that number of airworthy machines.

Since none of these aircraft had ever been intended as combat aircraft by their designers, turning them into combat machines was a formidable task. In the pre-independence days, however, their main role was reconnaisance and liaison, so that the lack of armament was of little consequence. But when independence came, the Sherut Avir was in an unenviable position. Opposing their 28 civilian light planes were five air forces equipped, to some degree or another, with modern combat aircraft. The Egyptian Air Force had 40 fighters, 10 bombers and 20 transports; the Iraqui, Syrian, Jordanian and Lebanese forces were far inferior in numbers but, even so, the Arabs could field 74 combat machines, 29 transports and 28 other aircraft between them, which gave them overwhelming numerical air

superiority. This was as apparent to the Arabs as to the Israelis and, indeed, one of the first Arab acts of the war was an air raid on Tel Aviv in which the airfield was a prime target and in which half the Sherut Avir's machines were damaged.

The remaining machines were rapidly dispersed and concealed, so, in spite of further air raids, there were no more losses, while the damaged machines were rapidly repaired and put back into service. The Arab air strength was then damaged by their own incompetence. They attacked a British airfield on which two RAF squadrons were still stationed to cover the final withdrawal of British troops, and British Spitfires promptly shot down several Egyptian aircraft.

Now the Sherut Avir's unarmed reconnaissance and liaison aircraft — the latter the first of 17 to arrive from the USA — were pressed into combat duties; the Dragon Rapide and a Norseman aircraft were both fitted with primitive bomb racks, while the Austers and Taylorcrafts turned themselves into bombers by the simple expedient of getting the co-pilot to throw hand grenades and home-made bombs out of the cockpit. Against an enemy not expecting air attack, a low night-time swoop by a quiet Auster showering grenades could be extremely demoralising, even if not particularly destructive in material terms.

The Sherut Avir was now reinfored by 20

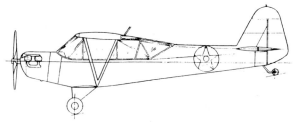

Piper Cub light airplanes, the American equivalent of the British Auster. These went to work ferrying men and supplies, making reconnaissance flights, and bombing by the out-of-the-cockpit technique. In spite of the paper superiority of the Egyptians, the light planes survived. The Egyptians learning the same lesson which US and British pilots had learned during the war, that Austers and Piper Cubs were not such easy meat for fast fighters as might be thought. The usual method of evading Arab Spitfires was to dive for the ground, pick some object such as a tree or house, and then fly round and round it in tight circles which the high-speed fighter could not match. The light planes used less fuel, so they could continue to fly their tight circles until the fighter, wasting fuel by the minute, gave up and flew home. An alternative trick, which demanded cool nerves, was to dive straight for the ground and pull out at the last minute. The pursuing fighter, much faster but less agile, usually failed to pull out and slammed into the ground. This trick had to be judged very precisely, though; if the dive was too prolonged, there was always the chance that the pursuer could get into position and shoot the light plane down before it was low enough to perform its escape manoeuver.

On 27 May 1948 the Sherut Avir was formally disbanded, and the official Israeli Air Force took its place. Known as Chel Ha' Avir, the Israeli Defence Force/Air Force is an independent service but is closely linked with the army through the General Staff. While perhaps offensive to air force purists, this system is the most appropriate one in Israeli circumstances, because of the vital importance the Israelis place on an integrated defensive structure. Despite various theories, history tends to show that totally independent air forces actually accomplish remarkably little unless their activies are geared to those of ground forces or fleets. Strategic bombing far behind the front may, in the long term, have some effect on the outcome of a prolonged war, but in Israel's position there is not time to wait for such an effect to filter through; the prime target is the one confronting the ground troops or threatening them. Very wisely, the Israelis therefore turned their faces away from the 'blue sky' school of air strategy and developed their air arm as a tactical rather than as a strategic weapon.

The formal establishment of the Chel Ha' Avir made very little difference to the actual conduct of the War of Independence, however. The new force merely inherited the same machines and men and continued to use them in the same way. However statehood did confer some advantages; it meant that now Israel could go out and buy aircraft — provided it could find the machines it wanted and persuade the owner to sell them. As the Chel Ha' Avir came into being, so it acquired

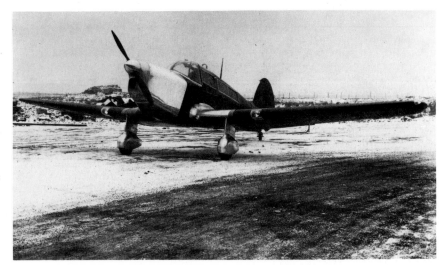

its first new aircraft. This was a Douglas Dakota DC3 transport, which was immediately converted into a makeshift bomber. Shortly after this, the first 'real' fighters began to appear.

These were not really what the Israelis wanted, but were simply all that was available to them. In fact, they were the result of a peculiar sequence of events in Czechoslovakia. During the Second World War the Czech Avia factory had been manufacturing Messerschmitt fighters for the German Luftwaffe, and continued manufacture for the benefit of the infant Czech Air Force after the end of the war. Unfortunately the factory producing the specified Daimler-Benz engines was destroyed by fire and very little could be salvaged. The Czech designers therefore turned to the Junkers Jumo as an alternative engine. This had been designed for use in Heinkel bombers and there was an ample supply stockpiled. With some difficulty they were fitted into the Messerschmitt airframe to produce the Avia S-199. The replacement engine was about two-thirds the power of the original, slower-running and much heavier, and its effect on the handling on the aircraft was near-lethal, especially during landing and take-off. Despite these drawbacks, the machines were acquired prior to independence, and in April 1948 ten were bought, with an option for 15 more. They could not be transported to Israel at that time, but pilots could be recruited and trained.

Avia S199 Mezek single-engined attack fighter, powered by Junkers Jumo 211F, producing 1,350hp. Speed 367mph, service ceiling 31,170ft, range (with 66gal drop tank) 528 miles. Armament two MG 151/20 cannon in wings and two MG131 13mm heavy machine guns in fuselage above engine.

Luftwaffe surplus The Czech Avia S199, the first true fighter to reach the infant Israeli Air Force, was an adaptation of the Messerschmitt Bf 109G. The enforced use of a Junkers engine, instead of the specified Daimler-Benz not only reduced performance, but made the airplane very difficult to fly — hence its nickname 'Mezek' (mule).

As soon as independence was declared, the S-199s started on their journey, the first four being dismantled and shipped in Curtiss Commando transports. On arrival they were rapidly reassembled and, on 29 May 1948, they flew their first combat sortie against an Egyptian armored column waiting to cross a damaged bridge near Ashdod on the road to Tel Aviv. One Avia was shot down, and another crashed on landing at its base, but the sudden attack so severely damaged the Egyptian column that it turned tail back towards Egypt, so relieving the pressure on Tel Aviv.

As more S-199s arrived, they were formed into a new unit, designated 101 Squadron, which was stationed at Ekron airstrip. From there they flew combat sorties in support of the army, and on 3 June the squadron commander, Modi Alon, shot down two converted Egyptian Dakotas which were bombing Tel Aviv. This was the first Israeli

success in air-to-air combat, and it put an end to Egyptian bombing raids as soon as the Egyptians realised that they were now up against something more than a handful of light planes.

The principal problem was the supply of aircraft; there was no shortage of pilots, since volunteers were flocking to Israel from all over the world. The majority of these were skilled pilots, who had flown for major air forces during the Second World War and who either espoused the Israeli cause or simply enjoyed combat flying. To obtain the machines with which to equip the pilots led to some far-fetched schemes and stratagems, however.

In Britain a gentleman announced that he was going to make a thrilling film about the bold New Zealand Air Force pilots who had flown the formidable Beaufighters during the war. The 'Beau' was a potent machine — once described as 'two large engines followed closely by an aircraft' —

armed with four 20mm cannon and six machine guns and capable of carrying rockets and bombs. The aircraft were acquired, and the producer decided that the scenery in the north of Scotland would be an excellent stand-in for the sequences of the film showing training in New Zealand. The Beaufighters took off accordingly, but never arrived there, having mysteriously taken a wrong turning and landed in Tel Aviv instead. It might have been thought that the film producer would have then prudently vanished from the scene, but, astonishingly, he managed to talk his way out of the problem — even managing to acquire spare parts, engines and machine guns for the Beaufighters before his welcome ran out and he, too, returned to Israel.

In the USA, some Israeli representatives invented an airline, bought three Constellation airliners for it, and then spirited one out of the country to Panama. The American authorities, alerted by this, impounded the other two until the War of Independence was over, but the single escapee got to Israel and proved of immense value in ferrying weapons and ammunition there from Czechoslovakia. Another spurious airline, Service Airways, purchased nine Curtiss Commando transports and set about flying them out from an airport in New Jersey. One crashed en route but the others eventually reached Israel after a roundabout trip through Mexico, Dutch Guiana, Natal, Morocco, Tunisia and Sicily.

Agents in the USA also found and bought four Flying Fortress B17 bombers, which had been 'de-militarised' to be sold as transports. These left the USA for Puerto Rico, having filed flight plans

for Brazil, but, like all the others, 'lost their way' and wound up in Tel Aviv, having refuelled in the Azores and then called in on Czechoslovakia to pick up arms and munitions. On their flight from Czechoslovakia to Tel Aviv they detoured to bomb Cairo in passing.

The final acquisition during this period was of 50 Mark XVI Spitfires which the Czech government had bought from Britain. Since the Avia S-199s were few in number and almost as dangerous to the Israelis as they were to the Arabs, 50 of one of the greatest fighters in the world promised to solve the air combat problem at a stroke. The only problem lay in getting them from Czechoslovakia to Israel, since the Spitfire's fuel capacity gave the plane an effective endurance of only 975 miles or so. Permission had been obtained to land and refuel in Yugoslovia, but even this was too far, so the Spitfires had to have additional fuel tanks fitted to enable them to make this first leg of their journey. The first attempts gave trouble; not only did aircraft crash, but, due to a forced landing on the Greek island of Rhodes, the Israeli operation received considerable unwelcome publicity, with the result that the Yugoslavs rescinded their landing permission. An attempt was made to add even more fuel tanks, so as to make the trip to Israel in one flight, but the dangerously overloaded machines ran into a storm. Four turned back successfully, but two crashed, killing their pilots.

When the War of Independence ended the Air Force took stock of its position. Almost all the foreign volunteers were demobilised and left Israel to return to their homelands. The airplanes

Strategic bomber Though the infant Israeli Air Force's role was largely confined to ground support, four Boeing B17 Flying Fortress bombers were purchased. They remained in service until after the 1956 war, when they bombed Gaza.

Boeing B-17G Flying Fortress strategic bomber, powered by four Wright R-1820-97 Cyclones, each producing 1,200hp. Speed 287mph, service ceiling 35,000ft range with 6,000lb bomb load 2,000 miles (usual Israeli bombload twelve 500lb bombs). Armament 0.5in Browning machine guns, fitted in waist positions. After 1949, operated in maritime-reconnaisance role.

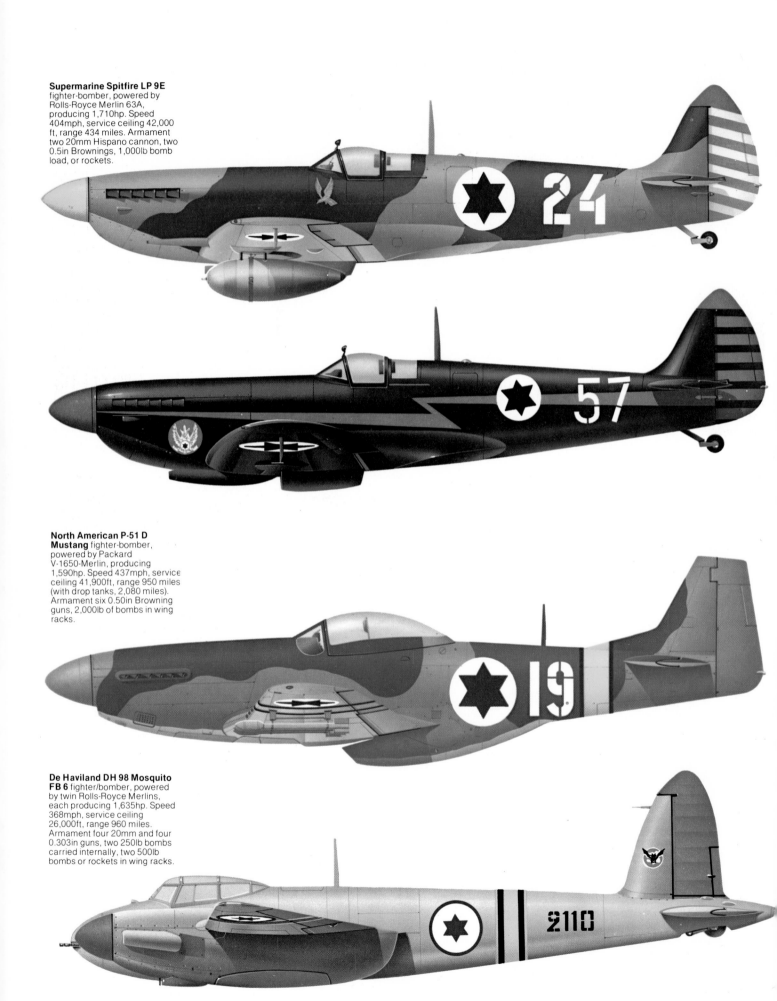

Supermarine Spitfire LP 9E fighter-bomber, powered by Rolls-Royce Merlin 63A, producing 1,710hp. Speed 404mph, service ceiling 42,000 ft, range 434 miles. Armament two 20mm Hispano cannon, two 0.5in Brownings, 1,000lb bomb load, or rockets.

North American P-51 D Mustang fighter-bomber, powered by Packard V-1650-Merlin, producing 1,590hp. Speed 437mph, service ceiling 41,900ft, range 950 miles (with drop tanks, 2,080 miles). Armament six 0.50in Browning guns, 2,000lb of bombs in wing racks.

De Haviland DH 98 Mosquito FB 6 fighter/bomber, powered by twin Rolls-Royce Merlins, each producing 1,635hp. Speed 368mph, service ceiling 26,000ft, range 960 miles. Armament four 20mm and four 0.303in guns, two 250lb bombs carried internally, two 500lb bombs or rockets in wing racks.

they left behind were a mixed collection, which had been brought together as opportunity offered without much thought for balance and most of them, in any case, were fit for nothing more than the scrap pile once the immediate emergency was over. The first priority therefore was to organize some suitable training aircraft and begin training pilots; the second was to weed out the force's aircraft and acquire new ones, this time with some degree of selectivity; and the third was to turn the air force into a disciplined branch of the armed forces. During the War of Independence, the foreign volunteers, good pilots though they undoubtedly were, had left a great deal to be desired as far as military discipline was concerned. They were not averse to 'bending' their orders in order to find something adventurous to do and, if their airstrip was short of ground transport, they usually solved the problem by going out and stealing the nearest jeep or truck. This had left the air force with a somewhat piratical reputation which it now had to live down.

Unfortunately the air force commanders during the post-war period had a hard row to hoe, principally because they were unable to make any impression on the politicians who held the purse-strings. The equipment they possessed was elderly before it arrived in Israel and was rapidly becoming obsolete by world standards, but the majority of the Knesset's members believed that the prime defence of Israel lay in the hands of the ground forces, so that whatever money was available was spent on tanks, artillery, machine guns and other similar requirements. No argument could convince them that air defence should be given at least equal priority. After two Air Force commanders had resigned in frustration at being regarded as arguing for a Cinderella service, the third was grudgingly authorized to

buy 25 Mustang fighters from Sweden and 60 Mosquito fighter-bombers from France in 1951; but, although these reinforcements were undoubtedly useful, they were still wartime designs, which were by now outclassed by the jets coming into service in the world's other major air forces.

In 1953 Dan Tolkovski became the commander of the Israeli Air Force. In the following year Egypt made its first arms agreement with Russia, with the result that the Egyptian Air Force was re-equipped with Soviet MiG-15 jet fighters. This unpleasant development gave Tolkovski his opportunity to do some straight and hard talking to the politicians, pointing out that, unless the Israeli Air Force was rapidly brought up to date, the next confrontation with the Arabs would end in aerial disaster.

Tolkovski took the air force by its heels and give it a thorough shaking-up. He realised that in the face of numerical superiority, only qualitative superiority had any chance of success, and he therefore set out to develop a force which was carefully tailored to suit its role and trained to the

Dog fight An Egyptian Spitfire circles in the sky above the smoke rising from Jaffa **(top)**, while **(above)** Ezer Weizman's Israeli Spitfire taxis for take-off. One of Israel's leading air aces, Weizman went on to become the Chel Ha'Avir's Chief of Staff and architect of Israel's air superiority.

The jet arrives The rugged twin turbojet Gloster Meteor was Israel's first jet fighter. Israeli modifications included fitting air-to-ground rockets and a rear-view cockpit canopy. The NF13's radar gave the young air force its first all-weather capability.

highest possible standards. The role, as he saw it, was firstly to destroy the enemy's air force, if possible on the ground, and then to give Israel's ground troops direct tactical support. Pure bombers, therefore, were unnecessary; there would be no long-range air raids. Similarly, pure fighters would be a luxury, since, once air superiority had been achieved, they would be relatively useless. What the Israeli Air Force needed, he believed, were multi-purpose fighters, fighter-bombers or fighter/ground attack machines which could be used for either air warfare or ground support interchangeably.

Another of Tolkovski's precepts was that the force had to be maintained in a constant state of air worthiness. A small air force could not afford to have machines out of action for a moment longer than was necessary, nor could it take its time about refuelling and rearming aircraft between sorties. Ground and maintenance crews were therefore given training as rigorous as that of the pilots, until they were able to repair aircraft and turn them round between sorties at speeds which astonished every other air force in the world, particularly Egypt's Soviet advisors.

The acquisition of modern Soviet jet fighters by the Arabs had aroused some concern in Britain and France and both countries now were prepared to reconsider their attitude to supplying Israel with arms. This was a fortunate step which coincided with Tolkovsi's appointment. After fierce argument, he had finally been able to reach agreement with David Ben-Gurion, the Prime Minister, over the air force's needs, and, in addition to some Gloster Meteor F8 jet fighters (ordered before Tolkovski's arrival), he was able to obtain Meteor NF13 fighters as well. These carried interception radar and so provided the Israeli Air Force with its first all-weather capability. From France, Tolkovski obtained Noratlas transports — large machines, whose extremely short take-off requirements were an extremely

useful asset to the Israelis with their short desert airstrips — and Dassault Ouragan jet fighters. These last, however, were a stop-gap order. What Tolkovski really wanted was the new Dassault Mystère IVA, but, since this was only in the design stage at the time, he was compelled to take the Ouragans in order to have a viable fighter force. Deliveries of the Ouragans began in 1955, with the first Mystères following the next year.

It was generally held that the Ouragan was a sub-standard machine, and would prove incapable of holding its own against the MiGs if it came to a dog fight. But when the 1956 war began this opinion rapidly changed; the Ouragan proved itself to be a robust performer which, in the hands of the highly-trained Israeli pilots, could take on anything the Arab nations could put into the sky and survive. In one air battle, two Ouragans were trapped by a flight of eight Egyptian MiGs; in spite of being hit by cannon fire both managed to out-manoeuvre their opponents until two Israeli Mystères arrived on the scene.

The Ouragan's strong suit was ground attack, and so it became the air force's principal weapon against enemy armor. Armed with four 20mm Hispano cannon and 16 rockets or two 450kg bombs, it could inflict severe damage on the lightly-armoured top surfaces of Egyptian tanks and could practically destroy anything less well protected. On one occasion two Ouragans even attacked the Egyptian destroyer *Ibrahim-el-Alwal* with considerable success; the ship was also engaged by naval forces and the result of this cooperation was its capture by the Israeli Navy.

Nevertheless, it should be stressed that, although the Ouragan could survive a meeting with the MiG 15, its survival was principally due to the superlative skill of the Israeli pilots. In itself, the aircraft was technically outmatched. The Chel Ha'Avir relied more upon the Dassault Mystère for actual air combat during the 1956 war. The first delivery of these began shortly before the outbreak of war, and 16 were in service throughout it. They distinguished themselves even in that short time, being credited with the shooting down of one MiG-17, three MiG-15s and four Vampire jets of the Egyptian Air Force, all without combat loss to the Israelis.

The Mystère had been developed by Dassault as a swept-wing successor to the Ouragan. Model IVA had a maximum speed of 685mph (1120km/hr) and was armed with two 30mm DEFA cannon and four wing pylons which could carry a variety of armament, including 450kg bombs and rockets. In Israeli service two of these pylons were usually taken to carry external drop tanks to give the aircraft a greater patrol range, but, even with this theoretical disadvantage, they were still capable of shooting down Egyptian jets. The 30mm DEFA cannon, developed jointly by

The French connection
The Dassault Ouragan fighter/bomber was the first of Israel's many purchases from France. The airplane was particularly suited to the ground attack role, causing havoc among the Egyptian armor at the time of Suez. It carried sixteen rockets or two 1,000lb bombs **(below)**.

Sea strike The Ibrahim el Alwal, formerly HMS Cottesmore (a Royal Navy 'Hunt' class destroyer) is towed into Haifa on 1 November 1956 **(above left)**. The air force played a vital role in the ship's capture, its Ouragan bombers disabling it so that the navy could step in. The Egyptian captain **(above)** steps ashore into captivity.

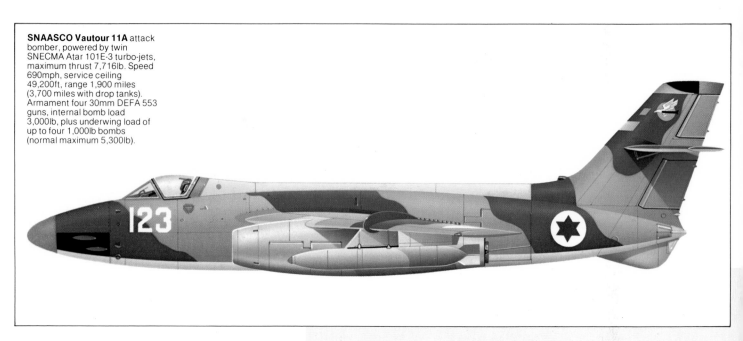

SNAASCO Vautour 11A attack bomber, powered by twin SNECMA Atar 101E-3 turbo-jets, maximum thrust 7,716lb. Speed 690mph, service ceiling 49,200ft, range 1,900 miles (3,700 miles with drop tanks). Armament four 30mm DEFA 553 guns, internal bomb load 3,000lb, plus underwing load of up to four 1,000lb bombs (normal maximum 5,300lb).

Britain and France from a German wartime design was found to be far more effective than the earlier 20mm Hispano cannon, due to its larger weight of shell and hence its greater destructive power. Because of the high manoeuvering speeds of the aircraft involved, the opportunities to actually fire a shot in modern aerial combat are brief, and this means that the few hits achieved must be as destructive as possible; the DEFA soon showed its superiority in this respect.

The 1956 war also saw the last appearance of some of the Chel Ha'Avir's older aircraft. The ex-Swedish piston-engined Mustangs suffered a high rate of attrition. Though Tolkovski's training of maintenance crews paid off — five were back in action within less than a day — they were now too slow and vulnerable and were disposed of as soon as the war was over. Similarly the now-ancient B-17 Flying Fortresses, which had survived since the War of Independence, were too slow and cumbersome to be flown in the face of modern MiG fighters. Though they escaped war damage — they were used to bomb Gaza — they were pensioned off shortly afterwards.

Irrespective of the effect of the 1956 war on Israel's political fortunes, it certainly had an effect on the fortunes of Chel Ha'Avir. The support the air force gave the ground troops, and also their prompt suppression of Arab attempts to dominate the sky over Israel, and the army in the field, made it obvious that air strength was a vital factor in the defence of Israel. Moreover, it was slowly becoming apparent that, in the future, the Israelis could not afford to wait until they were attacked; they needed to develop the capability of the pre-emptive attack, not as a purely aggressive strategy but as a de-fuzing tactic. As and when intelligence sources reported the presence of an at-

tacking force preparing to invade Israel, the use of a striking force to attack the attackers before they were ready to move would throw the enemy off balance and deprive him of the initiative. It was this line of argument which led to the coining of the phrase 'pre-emptive strike'. Furthermore, the best, indeed almost the only, vehicle for conducting a pre-emptive strike is the airplane. Missiles could be used, it is true, but only the piloted airplane can operate with surgical precision to cut the heart from the attacker, without wasting effort on inessentials.

This strategic rethinking meant that money suddenly became available and the air force quickly became popular. An analysis of the 1956 war was conducted, together with a review of the aircraft types in service and available, and it was decided that the first purchase would be an aircraft capable of acting as fighter and also as attack bomber. At the time, this left a limited range of options open to the Israelis and the airplane they chose almost selected itself; it was another French design, the SNCASO Vautour. Although perhaps little known, this was one of the best French developments of the 1950s, being large enough to carry an impressive payload but fast and nimble enough to be able to take care of itself in air combat. Flying at a speed of 680mph (1100km/hr), it carried four 30mm DEFA guns and had internal bomb racks for three 450kg or six 340kg bombs, plus underwing pylons for another four 450kg bombs.

In the Negev As tension builds in May 1967, a single-seater Vautour fighter-bomber swoops low over Israeli Centurions in the southern Negev.

Israel now had a stroke of luck. The French Air Force had ordered 300 single-seat Model IIA Vautours, but, for reasons best know to itself, cancelled the order after 30 had been built and accepted none of them. Since the manufacturers needed an alternative customer Israel was able to buy 18 at a very good price for delivery in 1957-8. It later bought four Model IIBRs, fitted with cameras, infra-red and radar sensors for reconnaissance, and eight Model IIN night fighters, one of which was specially fitted with electronic jamming equipment.

The next requirement was for a training aircraft for the new generation of jet pilots. The demise of the Mustang had convinced the Israelis that the day of the propeller-driven fighter was definitely over and that Israel must now equip itself with an all-jet force. This, in turn, meant the introduction of a comprehensive training and re-training program. The machine selected for use as the jet trainer was another French design, the Fouga Magister. At this time (1956) the Bedek Aviation Company of Israel (now Israeli Aircaft Industries Ltd.) was contemplating the manufacture of a modern aircraft, hoping to establish the foundations of a native industry. Arrangements were therefore concluded with the Fouga company for a license to build the Magister in Israel. The first dozen or so Magisters were bought from France, but thereafter assembly took place in Israel, with more and more components coming from local sources, until, by the late 1960s, the complete aircraft was being made and assembled in Israel.

The Magister had been chosen not simply because it was a good trainer, but because it was one of the first trainers with a sufficiently high performance to be used as a combat aircraft should the need arise. It could carry weapons and was capable of flying on ground attack missions. Maximum speed was 400mph (650km/hr), and the normal armament was two rifle-caliber machine guns in the nose, plus pylons under the wings for two 50kg bombs, two AS-11 anti-tank missiles, or two pods each carrying 18 37mm rockets. The Israeli-built version also incorporated a number of changes from the original French specification, these being designed and developed by Chel Ha'Avir experts to better suit the machine to Israeli conditions and uses. These include major structural change, with the incorporation of glass-fiber reinforced plastic in place of metal in the fuselage, while over 200 engineering modifications have improved maintainability, reliabilty and functioning.

In 1958 the Egyptian Air Force took delivery of MiG-19 fighters from Russia. These were supersonic — the MiG-19 was capable of Mach 1.3 at 20,000 feet — and were armed with three Nudelman-Suranov NS30 30mm cannon. These high velocity weapons, though of the same caliber as the DEFA gun, fired a projectile of twice the latter's striking energy. It was obvious that Israel had to re-equip its air force quickly with a supersonic fighter, but the choice was limited. The USA still would not sell modern warplanes to Israel, the British were in the throes of designing something suitable for their own use and had nothing available, leaving only the French. Fortunately Marcel Dassault, the designer of the Ouragan and Mystère, was never a man to rest on his laurels and had a suitable supersonic machine in production — the Super Mystère.

The Super Mystère was a successor to the Mystère IVA and, indeed, used many of its components. It differed in being larger and more powerful, being able to achieve a speed of Mach 1.125 (855mph) at its service altitude of 12,000m. It was armed with two DEFA 552 guns, improved versions of the original DEFA but still not as potent as the Soviet NS30, and could carry up to a ton of bombs, rockets or missiles under its wings. The French Air Force ordered 180, and, at the end of that production run, a further 24 were built for Israel. These were delivered in 1959; another 12 were bought from the French Air Force in 1963.

The superiority that the Super Mystère preserved for Israeli aviation soon appeared to be in danger once again. In 1958 the Soviets introduced the MiG-21 into service. By 1959, they were supplying it to China, and there seemed little doubt that their Middle Eastern allies would receive the plane in due course. This was a cheerless prospect for the Israelis to face. The MiG-21 could exceed a speed of Mach 2.0 (1,486mph), carried two NS30 cannon, or a gun-pack with a 23mm multi-barrel cannon, and had a payload of a ton of bombs or missiles.

Faced with this prospect, the Israelis decided that, instead of scouring around bargain basements for cast-offs, they were going to have to face the cost and buy the best supersonic multi-role fighter they could find. This meant going back to Marcel Dassault to purchase his latest creation, the Mirage III. This was an extremely agile and manoeuverable delta-winged fighter, capable of Mach 2.2 (1,635mph), and armed with two 30mm DEFA guns and either three air-to-air missiles or two 450kg bombs. The French Air Force were waiting for their first deliveries when the Israelis appeared on the scene, but, after much discussion and political dealing, the Chel Ha'Avir was permitted to buy 72 of the IIICJ variants in 1961. The C indicated that the plane was the interceptor version, and the J meant Jewish, reflecting the contribution of Israeli tests and suggestions to the final design. The price was high, but at last the Israelis had an aircraft which, on paper at least, was able to deal with anything the Arabs and their Soviet backers could produce. At the

Mikoyan MiG-17 Syrian multi-role fighter, powered by Klimov VK-1F turbojets, maximum thrust 7,452lb (with after-burners). Speed 711mph, service ceiling 54,460ft, maximum range (with drop tanks) 913 miles. Armament three 23mm cannon, four 550lb bombs.

Mikoyan MiG-19 Syrian multi-role fighter, powered by twin Tumansky RD-9B turbojets, maximum thrust 7,165lb (with afterburners). Speed 902mph, service ceiling c.40,000ft, range (with drop tanks) 1,366 miles. Armament three 30mm cannon, two air-to-air missiles, two rocket pods or two 550lb bombs.

Fouga Magister CM 170 trainer and light attack airplane, powered by twin Turbomeca Marbore IIA turbo-jets, or Marbore VI, maximum thrust 880lb and 1,058lb respectively. Speed 440mph, service ceiling 36,000ft, range (with wing-tip tanks) 575 miles. Armament two 7.62 guns in nose, plus underwing racks for two 110 bombs or two AS 11 missiles, or two pods containing 18 37mm caliber rockets.

Dassault Super Mystère SMB. 2 fighter/bomber, powered by Atar 101G-3 turbojet, maximum thrust (with afterburner) 9,833lb. Speed 739mph, service ceiling 55 775ft, range 540 miles. Armament Two 30mm DEFA 552 guns, wing pylons for 2,205lb of bombs or rockets (including two AIM-9 Sidewinder air-to-air missiles), 35 SNEB 68mm rockets carried in belly.

Missile attack The picture sequence here shows the destruction of an Egyptian MiG-19 by a Matra Magic air-to-air missile fired from an Israeli Mirage. In the picture **(top)**, the missile can be seen as a spot of light just above the cockpit; in the picture **(center)** it strikes and explodes; in the picture **(bottom)** the Mig breaks up. This dogfight on 29 November 1966 was the first time the missile had been used in combat.

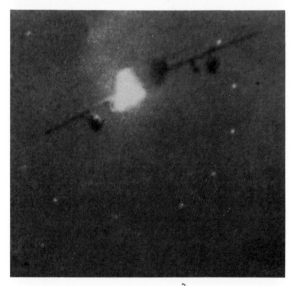

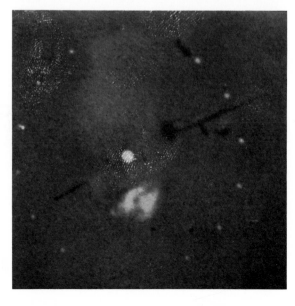

time, though, since the performance of the MiG-21 was not fully known, there was no assurance that the Mirage's performance would, in fact, better it. Indeed, the whole Mirage deal was a pig in a poke in many respects, since the contract was signed before the design had been fully perfected. But it was to pay off handsomely.

Having gained some experience with the first Mirages, the Israelis went back to Dassault and suggested a modified version. The original Mirage IIICJ was an all-weather machine, amply provided with radar and electronics; the Israelis now suggested a clear-weather version, removing the radar and electronics, so allowing more fuel and armament to be carried. The French company accepted the idea and so the Mirage V was born, with an Israeli order for 50. By the time the planes were ready for delivery, however, the French political climate had suffered one of its periodic changes of direction, since President de Gaulle had decided to side with the Arabs. He forbade further delivery of armaments to Israel, so the Mirage Vs were never delivered, even though the Israelis had paid for them in advance. After some argument the money was refunded to Israel, but Dassault went on building Mirage Vs for other customers. Ironically 110 were sold to Libya, of which a number were later transferred to Egypt to be used against Israel in 1973.

While still smarting from the French about-face, the Israelis now had a further stroke of good fortune. In 1962-3 Russia had begun delivering MiG-21 fighters to Egypt in order to balance the Israeli purchase of Mirages, the same machines being supplied to other Arab countries at a later date. In August 1966, however, an Iraqui pilot defected to Israel, bringing his MiG-21 with him. The defector was suitably rewarded and the Chel Ha'Avir soon began flying its prize for evaluation, including mock battles with its own Mirages. The evaluation dispersed all the mystery surrounding the Soviet machine, since it proved that it was somewhat underpowered and of limited range, though it was certainly agile in the sky. Extensive practice soon enabled Israeli pilots to develop tactics suitable for dealing with the MiG.

The years after the 1956 war also saw the introduction of several less glamorous, but equally vital, aircraft into the ranks of the Chel Ha'Avir. The 1956 campaign had revealed Israeli's need to transport troops rapidly and a number of helicopters were bought for this purpose. The first purchases were of the French Frelon type but these were underpowered for desert conditions, where heat and air conditions make helicopter operation particularly difficult. The more powerful Super Frelon was a better machine, but the majority of helicopters were purchased from the USA. Liaison aircraft to replace the Piper Cubs and Austers were needed, leading to purchases of the American Cessna 185 Skywagon and the Swiss Pilatus Super Turbo-Porter; the latter was particularly useful since, having been developed to operate at high altitudes in the Alps, it could cope well with the thin air of the desert.

Larger transports were also on the shopping list and the Israeli choice was the American Lockheed C-130 Hercules. But, despite the fact that they had sold helicopters and light airplanes to Israel, the US Government decided that C-130s were warplanes and refused to supply them. Just at that time, however, Israeli Aircraft Industries Ltd received two Boeing Stratocruiser airliners as part settlement of the debts of a bankrupt carrier. Knowing of the air force's requirements for large transports, the company suggested rebuilding them to military specification. The Chel Ha'Avir were not particularly impressed with the idea, having had enough of second-hand made-over makeshifts, but with no Hercules to be had, they accepted the offer. The IAI later acquired another 12 airliners from Pan-American Airways and converted them as well. The result was an extremely serviceable machine; the floors were strengthened for cargo carrying, clamshell doors were fitted in the rear, mechanized cargo handling equipment was fitted, and seats for paratroopers. Two aircraft had swing-aside tail units fitted, so that oversized loads could be got on board. In later years, more planes were acquired, some of them being converted into flight-refuelling tankers and others into electronic countermeasures carriers.

In the summer of 1967 the war clouds once again gathered over the Middle East, as Arab bellicosity found expression in a variety of sabotage attacks, guerilla raids, border incidents, and, finally, the eviction of UN peacekeeping observers from Sinai by the Egyptians and their closure of the Straits of Tiran to Israel-bound shipping. Announcing the closure, President Nasser said 'Israel does not today have Britain and France as she did in 1956. We stand face to face with Israel. The Jews threaten war, and we say to them "Welcome, come forth".'

The Arab forces were formidable, and burning to avenge the defeats of 1956. For the past decade the Soviets had been pouring munitions and technical advisers into the Arab countries and their armory was formidable. Egypt alone had 580 aircraft, of which 380 were fighters; the rest of the Arab consortium (Jordan, Syria, Iraq and the Lebanon) had 389 aircraft, of which 270 were fighters. The Israelis had 354 aircraft, of which 196 were fighters. On the ground the Egyptians alone had more armor than the German Wehrmacht had mustered to attack Frence in 1940. Waiting for the blow to fall was to court

disaster, and the Israeli General Staff decided that its only hope lay in their much-theorised 'pre-emptive strike'.

By this time Dan Tolkovski had been long retired and his place had been taken by Ezer Weizman, an ex-RAF pilot who had continued Tolkovski's policies and had built the Chel Ha'Avir up to its current strength. Weizman relinquished the post of C-in-C in 1965 to become head of Air Force Operations and was replaced by Mordecai Hod as C-in-C. Weizman now spent his time planning for the pre-emptive strike, and in 1967 his plans went into action.

The Chel Ha'Avir struck at 0745 hours on 5 June 1967. The plan called for a simultaneous attack on 10 Egyptian airfields, in accordance with Tolkovski's original concept of breaking the enemy's air strength first and then turning to ground support. The time was carefully chosen as being the moment when the Egyptians would least expect to be blitzed. Dawn, yes. Later in the morning, possibly. But 0845 (Egyptian time) was neither one thing nor another, and, as a result, the majority of the Egyptian pilots were breakfasting or driving to work in the heavy morning traffic. By coincidence two of the principal Egyptian commanders, Field-Marshal Ali Amer, the

Heavy flak The Arabs combine missile with conventional air defence. Here, PLO troops fire a Soviet ZPU-14 14.5mm multiple anti-aircraft gun at attacking Israeli jets.

First strike Helicopters burn on an Egyptian airfield after the Israeli pre-emptive strike in June 1967 **(below left)**, a complete triumph for air force commander Brigadier-General Mordechai Hod's strategy. Hod is seen alongside a

Mirage III fighter **(below right)**.

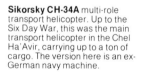

Sikorsky **CH-34A** multi-role transport helicopter. Up to the Six Day War, this was the main transport helicopter in the Chel Ha'Avir, carrying up to a ton of cargo. The version here is an ex-German navy machine.

Aérospatiale **Super Frelon SA 321K** transport and assault helicopter. It carries up to 9,921lb of cargo. The Israelis have modified these machines extensively; the one shown here is fitted with floats for amphibious duties.

Commander-in-Chief, and General Mahmoud Sidky, commander of the Air Force, had decided to conduct an inspection and were in the air between Cairo and Sinai at the time of the attack. In order to avoid the risk of an accident due to mis-identification, all Egyptian anti-aircraft batteries along their route had been given strict orders not to fire at any aircraft while the two commanders were airborne. In Sinai itself, all the senior Egyptian commanders had left their units to assemble at the airfield to greet their chiefs.

The attack was carried out by virtually every strike aircraft that the Israelis could muster, supported by ample fighter protection. The ground attack relied on Mystères, Super Mystères, Ouragans and Vautours, with Mirage fighters acting as top cover. The attacking flights flew low and fast to avoid detection by Egyptian radar, but, as they approached their targets, they climbed so as to become visible on the radar screens. This was a deliberate maneouver, timed so as to give the Egyptian aircrews just enough time to run and board their machines but not enough for them to take off. Thus the pilots would be trapped and wounded or killed in their machines when the attacks took place.

The first waves of Israeli machines met virtually no opposition; the anti-aircraft batteries were silent in obedience to their orders, and the only Egyptian aircraft to be encountered were four trainers. These were promptly shot down. Nine of the target airfields were struck within 15 minutes of the scheduled time, each being subjected to three or four passes in which cannon fire and bombs destroyed virtually every aicraft on the ground. The tenth field, Fayid, was shrouded in mist and the Israeli pilots had trouble finding it, though the delay in attack made no difference to the end result.

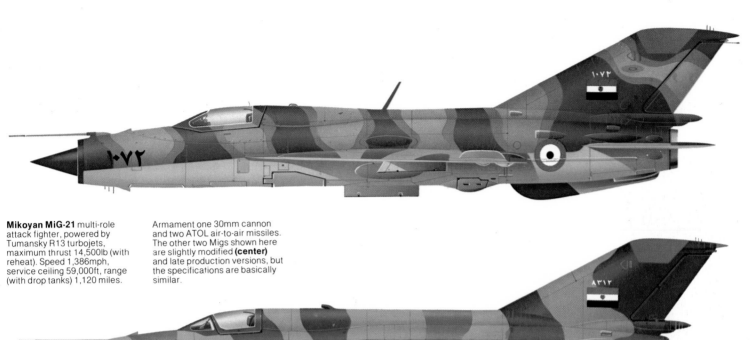

Mikoyan MiG-21 multi-role attack fighter, powered by Tumansky R13 turbojets, maximum thrust 14,500lb (with reheat). Speed 1,386mph, service ceiling 59,000ft, range (with drop tanks) 1,120 miles.

Armament one 30mm cannon and two ATOL air-to-air missiles. The other two Migs shown here are slightly modified **(center)** and late production versions, but the specifications are basically similar.

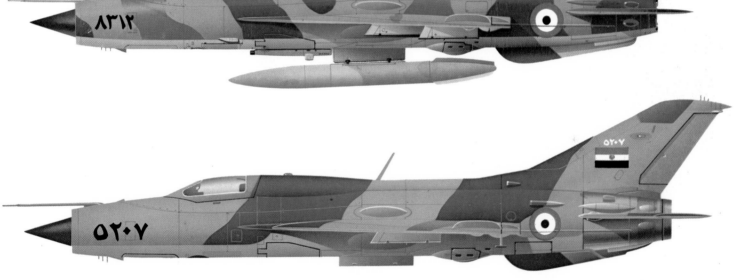

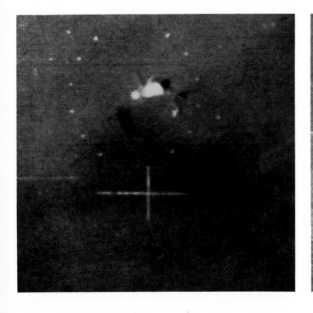

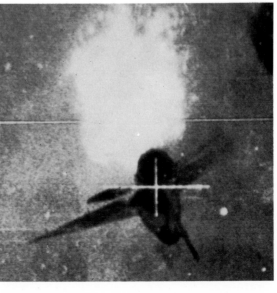

Wings above Suez These Israeli camera-gun pictures **(left)** show an Egyptian MiG-21 being hit by cannon fire, exploding and falling into the Gulf of Suez. Even advanced versions of the Mig posed little threat to Israeli air superiority.

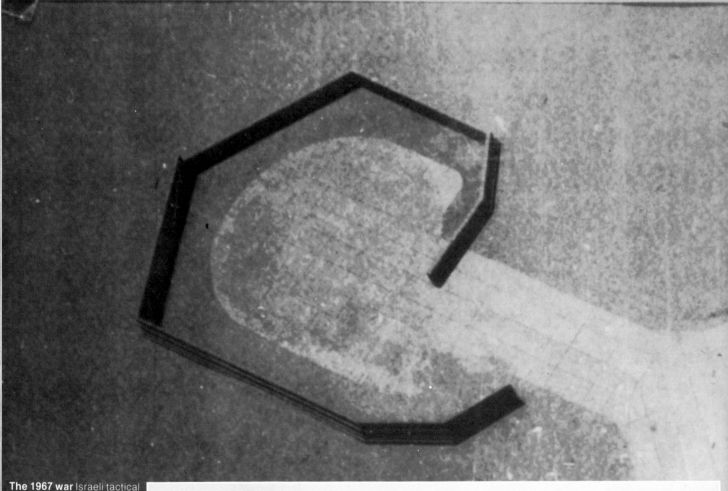

The 1967 war Israeli tactical airstrikes on Egyptian airbases during the opening hours of the 1967 war were a complete success, as the picture of a burning Tupolev heavy bomber demonstrates **(above)**. Even news agencies nod — this has been wrongly captioned as a Sukhoi SU-7 fighter on the photograph. Even after this success the Chel Ha'Avir did not relax its vigilance: a flight of Mirage III fighters keep a watchful eye out for signs of enemy activity as they patrol **(right)**. The Israeli censor has painted out the squadron markings on the nearest airplane.

Sukhoi 7' fighter bomber
air attack. (Army) (UPI)

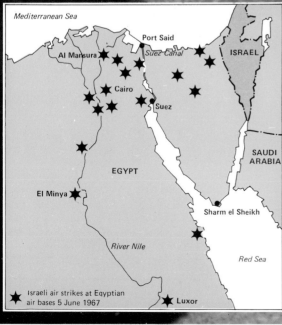

Dawn strike The map here shows the pre-emptive air strikes carried out against Egyptian air bases during the first two days of the 1967 war. Over 1,000 sorties were flown and around 300 Egyptian airplanes destroyed.

Mediterranean Sea
Port Said
Al Mansura
Suez Canal
ISRAEL
Cairo
Suez
SAUDI ARABIA
EGYPT
El Minya
Sharm el Sheikh
River Nile
Red Sea
★ Israeli air strikes at Egyptian air bases 5 June 1967
Luxor

As the first wave turned and made for home, so the second wave was coming in, some 10 minutes separating the two attacks. The perfection of the organization was such that, as the second wave struck, the third was well on its way, with the fourth taking off and the ground crews awaiting the return of the first. This, on its arrival, was refuelled, re-armed and turned round to become the fifth wave, striking some 50 minutes after its first attack. This pattern was kept up for almost four hours, by which time almost every plane in Nasser's air force was damaged or destroyed. Cannon fire accounted for most of the aircraft, which, since they were parked wing-to-wing on their airstrips with no attempt at concealment or dispersal, were an ideal target.

One of the surprises also unfolded by the Israelis was their employment of the 'dibber' bomb to disrupt airfield runways. This was a special bomb with a heavy pointed nose, fitted with parachute brakes and rocket motors. Once released, it fell through the air for a pre-determined distance, after which a parachute deployed to slow its flight, allowing it to turn in the air until it pointed downwards. At this point, the rocket motors ignited and the parachute was released, with the result that the bomb was now propelled at high velocity straight into and through the concrete apron of the airfield. It passed into the ground underneath and then detonated, producing an earthquake effect which ripped out huge slabs of concrete and left enormous craters in the runways. Some of the bombs were fitted with delay fuzes so that they came to rest in the ground but did not detonate for up to three or four hours afterwards. This normally coincided with the arrival of repair crews, who were vainly trying to fill in the craters. The effect of the explosion of the delayed action bombs was enough to send the maintenance men running for their lives. Naturally, they were then reluctant to approach the runways until they could be sure they were cleared of bombs, which meant that the Egyptians could undertake very little effective repair work for three or four days.

With the initial phase of the attack completed, the Chel Ha'Avir planes now turned round and began similar raids on another seven Egyptian airfields, further from the Nile Delta and so of secondary importance. After that, the planes took to the skies yet again, this time to deal with airfields in Jordan and Syria. By this time, of course, the Egyptians had gathered their wits and had begun to fight back; anti-aircraft fire accounted for some Israeli planes, but the Soviet SA-2 guided missiles deployed to defend Egypt against precisely this threat completely failed to deter it. Damage was so severe that few Egyptian aircraft were able to take off to engage in aerial combat, and eight MiGs which did appear were

Dassault Mirage IIICJ day fighter/bomber, powered by SNECMA Atar 9B3 augmented turbojet, maximum thrust 13,288lb (with afterburner). Speed 1,386mph (Mach 2.1), service ceiling 55,775ft (supersonic), range (with external tanks) 820 miles.

Armament two 30mm DEFA 5-52 guns, two AIM-9 Sidewinder or Shafrir air-to-air missiles, or two 1,000lb bombs. The Mirage IIICJ **(below)** has a modern camouflage scheme and has been up-rated with the Atar 9C turbojet.

Mistress of the sky An Israeli fighter/bomber seen over Amman on the first day of the 1967 Six Day War. Having virtually destroyed the Egyptian air force, the Israelis could soon turn their air power to other fronts.

all shot down, for the loss of two Israeli Mystères.

By the afternoon of 5 June the Arab nations had lost some 350 aircraft. Henceforward the Israelis could safely turn their attention to striking virtually any Arab ground target — their strong points, armored columns, troop concentrations and the like — since there was little or no aerial opposition. One of the minor facets of Israeli tactics during the first day had been a complete news blackout on their radio; they left Egypt and Syria

to do the talking, and the result was a 'fog of war' which baffled even the Arab commanders themselves. The Israelis knew that, once the Arabs appreciated their losses, they would immediately appeal to the United Nations for a ceasefire, but, provided that the Arabs believed they were winning, there would be no such call. Therefore it was in the Israeli interest for the Arabs to remain in the dark as to the true state of affairs for as long as possible, so as to allow the IDF to do as much damage as it could. The general feeling was that it would be two days before the Arabs realised what their position was and three before they asked for a cease-fire. The prediction was pessimistic; it took three days before the truth sank into the collective Arab mind and a further three days of vituperative argument followed before a cease-fire was invoked. Certainly, due to the Israeli silence, the Arabs at home knew very little of what was happening at the battlefronts. Egyptian radio claimed vast Israeli air losses and said nothing about their own — indeed it is said that even President Nasser never realized he had lost virtually all his air force until several hours after the attack — while the Egyptian propaganda was believed by Egypt's allies to such an extent that both Jordan and Syria began moving their troops forward in the assumption that there was no Israeli Air Force left to oppose them. They were to be speedily disillusioned.

It has been claimed that the Six Day Way of 1967 was won in two-and-a-half hours by the Chel Ha'Avir; though this is a simplification, it has a good deal of truth in it. Not only had the preemptive strike proved its worth, but with such an immediate and resounding victory to the airforce's credit, the morale of the Israeli ground forces was so high as to almost literally propel them forward to smash all the opposing enemy forces. The end of the war, however, found Israel saddled with more liabilities than ever. She had conquered vast stretches of territory — the Golan Heights, the West Bank of the Jordan, and the Sinai up to the Suez Canal itself — and the army was stretched to occupy it. At the same time Soviet Russia rapidly replenished the Arab armories with fresh supplies of MiG-21 and Sukhoi Su-7 fighters, tanks, artillery and every other weapon imaginable, while, as a final blow, the

Booty from the battle Even the vaunted Soviet SA-2 anti-aircraft missiles provided the Egypians with little effective defence in the 1967 war. Here, a SA-2 battery captured in the Sinai is being removed for expert evaluation.

Sukhoi SU-7 attack fighter, powered by Lyulka AL-7F turbojets, maximum thrust 21,164lb (with reheat). Speed 1,055mph, service ceiling 49,200ft, range 900 miles. Armament two 30mm cannon, four bombs up to 5,470lb.

French cut off their supply of arms to Israel, since they regarded the Israelis as the irresponsible aggressors.

Enraged and humiliated by the result of the war, Nasser declared what he called a 'war of attrition' against the Israelis, shelling the Israeli troops in the Sinai, launching tip-and-run bombing raids against them and generally making life as uncomfortable as possible, without, of course, taking the final step to full-scale conflict. Israeli attempts to counter this policy of pin pricks by air counter-attacks placed a heavy burden on the air force, due to the vast reinforcements of anti-aircraft guns and missiles from Russia that the Egyptians positioned along the Suez Canal.

With the cessation of supplies from France as well, the Israelis began to feel the pinch. Their first move was to explore the possibility of building a modern fighter of their own, but this, even if it proved possible, would obviously take a considerable time. The only other countries producing aircraft capable of taking on the MiGs, and Sukhois were Sweden (the Saab Draken), Britain (the BAC Lightning) and the USA (Phantom and Skyhawk). Adhering to its strict policy of neutrality Sweden refused to provide any aircraft; Britain's Lightning had been designed to suit its own air defence system and did not possess the required range or the armament preferred by the Israelis. This left only the USA. The Americans previously had never been very helpful, but now, having observed the shifting balance of power in the Middle East, they had a change of heart and agreed to supply war material to Israel. This decision saved the day. F-4E Phantoms and A-4 Skyhawks were soon being shipped, together with C-130 Hercules transports and Sikorsky S-65 helicopters. All of these were machines the Israelis had coveted for a long time.

Experts have called the F-4E Phantom one of the greatest combat aircraft of all time. Larger than any previous fighter used by the Israelis — and at $4.5 million each certainly the most expensive — the combat performance of the Phantom had been proved in Vietnam and was far superior to that of any aircraft then in the Middle East. With a speed of Mach 2.2 (1,635mph), it was armed with a multi-barrel 20mm M61A1 Vulcan Gatling gun, capable of spewing out 3,000 shells a minute, plus four AIM-7 Sparrow air-to-air missiles recessed into the fuselage, another four AIM-9 Sidewinder missiles on wing pylons, a central pylon for a droptank or up to 1,350kg of bombs, and four wing pylons for another 5,800kg of bombs. This enormous payload gave the plane incredible versatility; it was capable of close-in combat with the cannon, 'stand-off' combat with the air-to-air missiles, and ground attack with gun and bombs.

The A-4 Skyhawk was another remarkably powerful air weapon. The Israelis regard this, too, as one of the best combat airplanes in existence. It can carry an enormous payload and yet remains astonishingly agile. Though its top speed is far below that of the F-4E — about 621mph (1000 km/hr) depending upon how heavily it is loaded — its manoeuverability makes up for this. In Israeli service, it is armed with two 30mm DEFA guns, while it can carry up to 7,250kg of armament on its wing pylons. Its greatest attraction lies in its simplicity, its easy of maintenance and its resistance to damage.

The war of attrition now began to escalate dangerously. The long-range ability of the F-4E allowed it to circle around the defended area of the Suez Canal and strike at targets inside Egypt. In desperation Egypt obtained new SA-3 missiles and ZSU-23 radar-controlled multiple anti-aircraft guns from Russia, complete with Russian 'advisors' to operate them. In a final bid for air supremacy, Egypt also obtained five squadrons of Soviet MiG-21 interceptors, complete, again, with Russian 'advisors'. In June 1970 Russian-flown MiGs finally came up against Israeli Skyhawks, Mirages and Phantoms and suffered bloody noses for their trouble. By this time, however, both sets of super-powers were becoming alarmed, and even Egypt was beginning to think she might have bitten off more than she could chew. The war of attrition finally came to an end with a cease-fire on 8 August 1970.

SA-6 in operation The Soviets responded to the Arab defeat in 1967 by providing them with the highly mobile and sophisticated SA-6 missile system, in which both radar and infra-red guidance are used to locate targets.

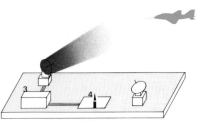
An enemy aircraft (1) is detected by radar (2). The information is fed to a computer (3), which

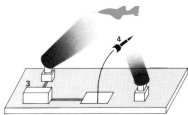
programmes the missile with launch instructions (4). The missile is launched and another ground radar (5)

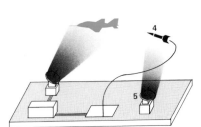
tracks the missile to steer it towards the target. In the last phase, the missile uses a heat-seeking mechanism

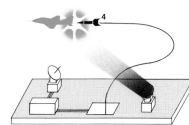
to guide itself onto the infra-red radiation from the target's jet exhaust.

Parade, practice and action Soviet missiles take pride of place in this Arab military parade **(above)**. Both SA-4 in the foreground and SA-6 beyond it were to have a devastating effect in the 1973 war. An Egyptian soldier **(left)** waves his shoulder launcher in jubilation, after scoring a direct hit with his SA-7 in a training exercise; the PLO guerilla **(right)** has just fired a SA-7 at an Israeli jet. Launcher and guerrilla are obscured by smoke, but the missile can be clearly seen.

Under attack This remarkable photograph shows an Israeli Mirage being attacked by a Syrian missile over Lebanon. The outcome of the encounter is not known, but the Israelis were quick to equip their airplanes with electronic countermeasures to deal with this new threat.
(Over page).

Showing the flag Israel suffered heavy air losses in the opening battles fo the 1973 war, but, despite them, the Chel Ha'Avir flew doggedly on, realizing the country's fate lay in its hands. Here, Israeli jets support Israeli ground forces on the Kuneitra-Damascus road.

Soviet aid A MiG-21 over Damascus. Even this most modern of Soviet jets could not overcome Israeli air superiority.

Protection SA-3 missiles provided the umbrella which protected the Egyptian crossing of the Suez Canal in the 1973 war.

Plane for plane Israel and the Arabs constantly battle for air superiority. Some of the types used by both sides since the 1940s are shown **(bottom)**, together with comparative performance and armament figures.

Israel's first task now was to replace its losses. France had already been asked for the Mirage V, designed to Israeli specification, but this source of supply had, of course, dried up. In response to the problem, Israeli Aircraft Industries now began examining the possibility of taking the American J-79 engine, which powered the Phantom fighter, and inserting it into the Mirage airframe to upgrade the Mirage's performance. This was something of a technical achievement, since the two engines had vastly different dimensions, but it was successfully accomplished. The refitted Mirages were known as Salvo.

At about the same time, Israeli secret agents managed to obtain blueprints of the French Atar 9C engine used in the Mirage, so it was possible for Israel to contemplate manufacturing its own engines. Soon afterwards, other agents in France laid their hands on the technical drawings of the Mirage III and Mirage V. The Israelis now possessed the complete plans of both engine and airframe and began building new Mirage IIIs secretly in Israel, calling them Nesher (Eagle). The first of these flew in 1971; since their external appearance was identical to the French-supplied Mirages, nobody outside the Israeli Air Force and Israeli Air Industries knew that an Israeli-manufctured version was in existence.

The next step was to combine the two programmes and fit the Nesher with the American J-79 engine. Again, this was a considerable engineering feat, but it was eventually perfected. The new airplane went into service in the summer of 1973 as the Barak (Lightning).

Finally, taking the drawings of the Mirage V and with the experience gained with both Nesher and Barak, the final task was to build the Mirage V airframe and put the J-79 engine into it. The result was to be called the Kfir (Lion Cub). Work began in 1971, but it proved to be a long, difficult job, since it took time to incorporate several modifictions which the air force considered essential in the light of its combat experience. Before Kfir was ready for combat, however, the Chel Ha'Avir was to be put to the test yet again.

While Israel was busy with its air force, the Arabs were planning their revenge for 1967. One of their prime areas of overhaul was their air defence system, and, with Soviet assistance, they developed a highly effective combination of guns and missiles, working together. During the 1967 war, the principal Egyptian anti-aircraft weapon had been the Soviet SA-2 missile, augmented later by the SA-3. The problem with the SA-2 is that it is a high-level defender, so the easy response is to fly below its minimum operational height; it was the use of this tactic by the Israelis which led to the Egyptians obtaining SA-3 to operate at lower altitudes. The Israelis, in turn, countered SA-3 partly by flying even lower and partly by obtain-

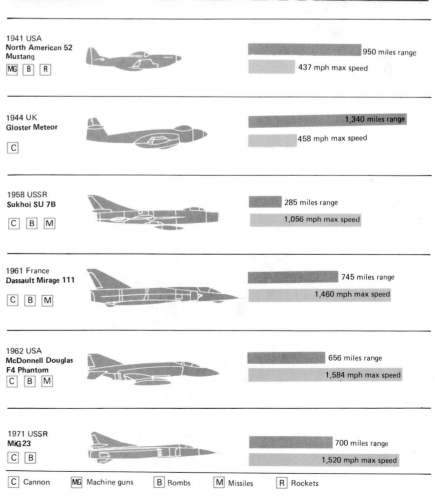

1941 USA North American 52 Mustang MG B R		950 miles range	
		437 mph max speed	
1944 UK Gloster Meteor C		1,340 miles range	
		458 mph max speed	
1958 USSR Sukhoi SU 7B C B M		285 miles range	
		1,056 mph max speed	
1961 France Dassault Mirage 111 C B M		745 miles range	
		1,460 mph max speed	
1962 USA McDonnell Douglas F4 Phantom C B M		656 miles range	
		1,584 mph max speed	
1971 USSR MiG 23 C B		700 miles range	
		1,520 mph max speed	

C Cannon　MG Machine guns　B Bombs　M Missiles　R Rockets

Air action An Israeli fighter shoots down a Syrian MiG-21 in an air battle. In this clash, the Israelis claimed they had destroyed seven MiGs without loss in a twenty-minute dogfight, fought at altitudes between 10,000 and 30,000 feet. Despite their losses at the start of the 1973 war, the Israelis soon reasserted their air superiority.

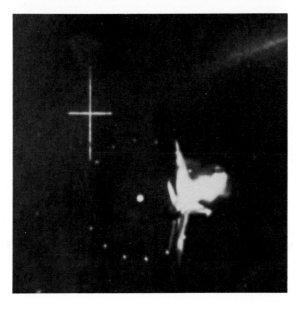

ing suitable electronic jamming equipment from the Americans, and then manufacturing their own.

The Egyptians were now supplied with SA-6 missiles. Not only do these possess a good low-level capability, but they also dispense with radar during the last part of their flight, homing on to the target by tracking the infra-red emissions from the aircraft's engine. Attempts to dodge SA-6 by flying lower brought Israeli planes into range of the ZSU-23 guns. These self-propelled radar-guided four-barrel 23mm cannon proved extremely lethal. Finally, army units were issued with SA-7 missiles; these were one-man weapons, fired from the shoulder, which homed on to the target by infra-red means. The SA-7 is, obviously, a short-range weapon, but together with the ZSU-23, it makes low flying an extremely hazardous proposition.

The result was that the entire airspace above the Egyptian positions was now protected. High-flyers were engaged with the SA-2, with the other weapons coming into play as the attacking aircraft flew lower and lower. There was no longer any safe altitude. Moreover, the SA-6 and ZSU-23 weapons had been used very sparingly during the war of attrition while the SA-7 was not used at all, so that the Israeli electronic 'ferrets' who flew close to the borders to pick up and analyze Egyptian radar signals to devise devices to jam them detected very few. Thus, no adequate electronic countermeasure was developed. Furthermore, electronic systems were useless against the infra-red homing capability of the two missiles.

As the Egyptians realized, the Israeli defence forces were highly trained for an aggressive form of defence. Their air force was strong in ground attack aircraft and their army was strong in armor, while the whole Israeli military philosophy was founded on the lightning thrust to disrupt the enemy and put him at a disadvantage. Therefore, the Arabs reasoned, let us adopt this tactic ourselves, placing the Israelis on the defensive, limiting our objectives and beating the Israelis down between the hammer of Egypt and the anvil of Syria. The one Israeli fear was of a protracted war, in which their weapons and supplies would be used up faster than they could be replaced, and it was precisely this the Arab nations now intended to bring about.

On the afternoon of 6 October 1973, the Israeli troops holding the Golan Heights were attacked by five Syrian divisions, mustering 1,500 Soviet T-62 tanks between them. Simultaneously, on the Sinai front, the Egyptian Army mounted a lightning attack across the Suez Canal. The initial success was overwhelming, since the Israelis were caught completely by surprise.

The Chel Ha'Avir went into action immediate-

McDonnell Douglas A-4E Skyhawk single-seat attack aircraft, powered by Pratt and Whitney J52 unaugmented turbojet, maximum thrust 8,300lb. Speed 674mph, service ceiling 42,250ft, combat range 385 miles. Armament two 30mm DEFA 552A guns, up to 8,200lb of ground attack armament and Shafrir air-to-air missiles. Specifications approximate, as there are many variants in service.

MacDonnell Douglas F-4E Phantom two-seater fighter and attack aircraft, powered by twin General Electric J79-GE-17 turbojets, maximum thrust 17,900lb (with afterburner). Speed 1,432mph (Mach 2.17), service ceiling 58,750ft, combat radius 306 miles. Armament 20mm M(1A1 gun, four AIM-7E-2 or Sparrow air-to-air missiles, two pairs of Shafrir or Sidewinder missiles, up to 16,000lb of bombs.

Air defence The US Sidewinder air-to-air missile is one of the most efficient in the world **(left)**. The Israelis have developed their own Shafrir variant.

Essential back-up A female mechanic and a male colleague service an A-4 Skyhawk between missions. As in the other services, women have an equally important role in the Israeli Air Force **(below)**.

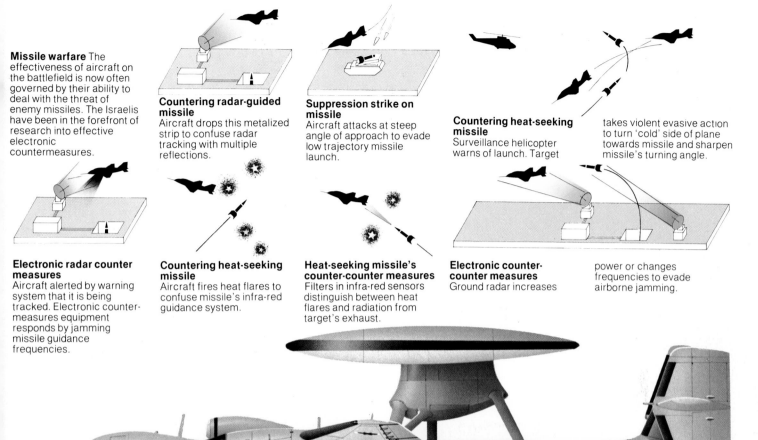

Missile warfare The effectiveness of aircraft on the battlefield is now often governed by their ability to deal with the threat of enemy missiles. The Israelis have been in the forefront of research into effective electronic countermeasures.

Countering radar-guided missile
Aircraft drops this metalized strip to confuse radar tracking with multiple reflections.

Suppression strike on missile
Aircraft attacks at steep angle of approach to evade low trajectory missile launch.

Countering heat-seeking missile
Surveillance helicopter warns of launch. Target

takes violent evasive action to turn 'cold' side of plane towards missile and sharpen missile's turning angle.

Electronic radar counter measures
Aircraft alerted by warning system that it is being tracked. Electronic countermeasures equipment responds by jamming missile guidance frequencies.

Countering heat-seeking missile
Aircraft fires heat flares to confuse missile's infra-red guidance system.

Heat-seeking missile's counter-counter measures
Filters in infra-red sensors distinguish between heat flares and radiation from target's exhaust.

Electronic counter-counter measures
Ground radar increases

power or changes frequencies to evade airborne jamming.

ly on both fronts, but the massive Arab air defence system now showed its teeth and the losses were enormous. Only the air force, however, could stave off the Arabs long enough to buy time for the remainder of the Israeli Defence Force to be mobilised and deployed, and the price was to be a stiff one. The obvious tactic was to launch aircraft ground attack against the Syrian armor and the Egyptian crossings over the Suez Canal; it was precisely this that the Arabs had planned and hoped for, and their air defences were deployed to take advantage of it. At the same time, the Arabs carefully held back their own air forces. They would rely entirely upon their anti-aircraft batteries to thin out the Israelis, so that, eventually, when the Israeli air strength was worn down, the Arabs would be able to assert immediate air superiority. The principal Arab air effort at the time was the raiding of Israeli air bases in an effort to destroy the maintenance and back-up services that kept the Chel Ha'Avir flying.

By the third day of the war the Egyptians were well across the Canal and the Syrians had taken most of the Golan Heights. The Israelis had lost some 50 first-line planes, but the sacrifice had allowed the ground forces to get into action and these were beginning to make an impression on the invaders. The Syrians were under counter-attack and being slowly pushed back, while the

Egyptians, reluctant to advance until their air defences moved forward, were being held in the Sinai.

On the fifth day the Soviets began to ferry more arms to the Egyptians and Syrians, and the Israelis began to feel the pinch; it was calculated that they had sufficient equipment and ammunition to fight for another seven days, after which their bolt would be shot and the Arabs would be able to advance virtually without opposition. However, the Soviet airlift eventually worked to the Israelis' advantage. The Americans, appalled by this blatant Soviet encouragement and aware of the Israelis' plight, suddenly opened their supply dumps and began supplying armaments to Israel as fast as they could. First-line aircraft were stripped from US Air Force units and flown directly to Israel, refuelling in-flight. US Marine Skyhawks were flown from aircraft carriers. Heavy transport aircraft arrived with tanks, artillery and ammunition. Most useful, though perhaps least publicised, was the supply of the American electronic countermeasures pods that had been developed to deal with SA-2 and SA-6 missiles in Vietnam. These were rapidly fitted to Israeli aircraft to give them some measure of protection, which was increased still further by the provision of American heat decoys to lead the infra-red homing missiles astray. Radiation-seeking missiles, which would fly down a radar

Grumman Hawkeye E2-C airborne early-warning surveillance, powered by twin Allison T56-A-425 turboprops. Speed 374mph, service ceiling 30,900ft, maximum endurance six hours six minutes. Equipped with General Electric APS-125 radar, ECCM (electronic counter-counter measures equipment) and digital MTI (moving target indication). Level of Israeli adaptation unknown.

Constant vigile The sleek profile of an A-4 Skyhawk high in the sky symbolizes the Chel Ha'Avir's constant readiness. The empty missile mountings suggest that the pilot is returning to base to rearm **(far left)**.

beam to destroy radar transmitters, were also supplied. With the help of all these, the Chel Ha'Avir began to dominate the Arab air defence system.

On the eleventh day of the war, the Israeli armored forces managed to cross the Suez Canal and establish a bridgehead on the Egyptian side. This was one of the turning points of the campaign. Once the Egyptians realised what had happened they launched their air force into the attack, but the Israelis were waiting and a series of fierce aerial battles began over the canal. The advancing Israeli ground forces had been reinforced and managed to overrun a number of the Egyptian missile batteries. This meant that there was now a missile-free corridor across which the Chel Ha'Avir could fly to attack air bases and other targets inside Egypt.

Air battles were now raging over all the front.

Israeli airplanes were shooting down Arab machines at an increasing rate, and it was not without interest that the Israelis discovered North Koreans, Cubans and Pakistanis featuring among the downed 'Arab' pilots. The latest Soviet Su-20 variable-geometry-wing fighters appeared on the Syrian front and were promptly shot down, as were two which attempted to raid Haifa. The Israelis had achieved definite air superiority in the face of enormous odds and at a terrible price, but the tide had turned. On 22 October a UN cease-fire was brought into force and the war finally ended two days later.

Altogether the Arabs had lost 514 aircraft, though 58 of these had fallen victim to their own anti-aircraft batteries. Similar losses had happened on the Israeli side as well, which was scarcely surprising since both sides were using Mirages. The Israelis had lost 102 aircraft — 53 Skyhawks, 33 Phantoms, 8 Mirages and 3 Super Mystères — about 40 of these being destroyed by ground missiles. In the Israeli postwar analysis, it was felt that a more single-minded attack on the Egyptian missile sites might have paid dividends, but, as was pointed out, the air force was carrying the entire burden of the war for its first two days and had to carry out whatever task it had been given. To have devoted itself solely to self-protection by taking out the missile batteries would have left the rest of the defence forces in a perilous position.

After the 1973 War, the Chel Ha'Avir set about rebuilding its force, notably by bringing the Kfir into service. In fact the Kfir turned out to be rather less agile than had been hoped, due to the choice of a delta wing configuration. The Kfir-2 was developed accordingly. This has tiny wing

Casualty In all wars, helicopters have a high attrition rate, as this picture of a crashed Sikorsky CH-53 demonstrates.

Sikorsky CH-53 heavy airlift helicopter, load 42,000lb (empty weight 23,485lb), range 257 miles. All Israeli models carry drop tanks and in-flight refuelling probes.

Ready to strike The Israeli-built Kfir is the logical development of the Mirage design, perfected by Israeli technology and an element of espionage.

Sukhoi SU-20 attack fighter, powered by Tumansky R-29B turbojets, maximum thrust 25,350lb (with reheat). Speed 1,430mph, service ceiling over 40,000ft, combat radius 530 miles. Armament two 30mm MR30 cannon, maximum 7,716lb of bombs or rockets.

Mikoyen MiG-23 attack fighter, powered by Tumansky R-29B turbojets, maximum thrust 25,350lb (with reheat). Speed 1,520mph, service ceiling 59,000ft, range 2,100 miles. Armament one 23mm cannon, two or four air-to-air missiles, depending on missile variant, or 9,920lb of bombs.

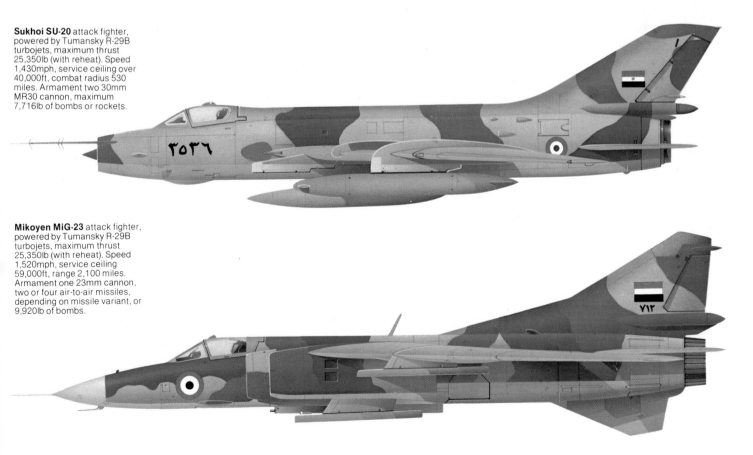

Renewed supremacy The first General Dynamics F-16 lands at an unidentified Israeli air base on 2 July 1980. This was one of four, the advance guard of a 75-plane order.

surfaces, known as 'canards', on the fuselage, above and ahead of the main wing, which makes the plane more manoeuverable.

The struggle for supremacy in the sky continues. As noted above, the 1973 war found Su-20 swing-wing fighters in Arab hands, and since that time they have acquired even more lethal airplanes. The MiG-23 and MiG-25 fighters, the latter the fastest operational fighters in existence with a speed of Mach 3.3 (2,451mph) and a ceiling in the stratosphere, were beyond the capabilities of any Israeli Phantom or Skyhawk to catch, let alone destroy. The Chel Ha'Avir therefore had to look to the Americans for the supply of their latest supersonic fighters in the effort to regain some sort of air parity.

The Americans, also alarmed by the performance of the MiG-25, had set about developing an answer to it. This was the F-15 Eagle, with a speed of Mach 2.5 (1,648 mph), and armed with a six-barrelled 20mm cannon, eight missiles and up to 7,250kg of bombs. Though not so fast in straight flight as the MiG-25, the F-15 is the better airplane, since the MiG is generally agreed to have no aerial combat ability, while the F-15 is a superlative all-rounder. Its size and staggering price led the Chel Ha'Avir to think long and hard before placing its order, but there was no other machine on offer in the early 1970s that appeared capable of anything like the same performance. 48 were ordered in 1975.

By that time, however, another possible aircraft had appeared — the F-16 Fighting Falcon.

Cheaper and smaller than the F-15, it is nevertheless a nimble and fast machine armed similarly to the former airplane, and in 1977 Israel cut back its order for F-15s to 25 and announced its intention to buy 75 F-16s. Another F-15 order was later placed — a further 15 of the improved F-15C being ordered in 1979 — after which a third order for another 11 was given. The first batch of F-16s having been delivered, a second batch of 75 ordered but, at the moment of writing, delivery has been embargoed as part of the US response to the Israeli invasion of the Lebanon.

Both the F-15 and F-16 have proved their worth in combat since their arrival. F-15s have scored numerous kills against Syrian intruders without loss, while eight F-16s each carrying two 900kg bombs flew almost 1,000km to bomb and destroy the Osirak nuclear reactor in Iraq in June 1981.

The Chel Ha'Avir has come a long way since its first sorties with Piper Cubs and Tiger Moths in 1947. It is, without any doubt, the most battle-experienced and combat-skilled air force in existence today; it is frequently asserted that the highest-scoring jet 'ace' in any air force is an Israeli, though his identity is secret. High quality training, motivation, and the best possible equipment have been brought together to produce a force which is without rivals and which, without any doubt, has saved Israel from disaster on several occasions. How the future will unfold remains to be seen, but whatever the state of affairs in the Middle East, the Chel Ha'Avir will be ready for it.

IAI Kfir C1 multi-role attack fighter, powered by General Electric J79-J1E augmented turbojet, maximum thrust 17,900lb. Speed 1,516+ mph (+Mach 2.3), service ceiling 58,000ft, combat range various, depending on payload, but between 215 and 417 miles. Armament two IAI DEFA 5-52 guns and 9,469lb additional armament including two Shafrir 2 air-to-air missiles, Luz-1 missiles, Maverick or Hobos missiles, ten 500lb bombs, rocket pods, Matra Durandal antai-runway weapon, napalm. The C2 version **(below)** is the production model, adapted to increase low-speed and combat manoeuvrability.

General Dynamics F-16A Fighting Falcon multi-role attack fighter, powered by Pratt and Whitney F100-PW-200 augmented turbo-fan, maximum thrust 23,830lb (with afterburner). Speed 1,350mph (Mach 2.05), service ceiling 50,000ft +, tactical radius 340 miles (without drop tanks). Armament one 20mm M16A-1 gun, two AIM-9L or Shafrir air-to-air missiles, additional armament load up to 20,450lb.

McDonnell Douglas F-15A Eagle attack fighter, powered by twin Pratt and Whitney F100-PW-100 augmented turbofans, maximum thrust 23,830lb (with afterburner). Speed 1,648mph (Mach 2.5), service ceiling 65,000ft, range 2,878 miles. Armament one 20mm M161A-1 six-barrel gun, four AIM-7F Sparrow air-to-air missiles, four AIM-9L or Shafrir air-to-air missiles, bombs or rockets up to 16,000lb.

The Israeli Army

THE NOMINAL PEACETIME STRENGTH of the Israeli Army today is 138,000 which includes 120,000 conscripts, both male and female. The strength rises to 375,000 upon mobilization.

The largest regular formation is the brigade. There are 20 armored brigades, of which five are maintained at full establishment, one is approximately half-strength, and the remaining 14 are at cadre strength. This means they have sufficient regular troops to ensure the maintenance of equipment and the continuity of administration. There are nine mechanized infantry brigades (four at half establishment, five at cadre strength) and nine infantry brigades (also split four and five), and five parachute brigades (two at full establishment, one at half, and two at cadre strength). There are also nine artillery brigades, the majority of which are at cadre strength.

The equipment used by this force is among the most heterogenous of any army in the world. It is obtained by a mixture of organised procurement and fortuituous aquisition, being mainly Western designs or locally-produced weapons, or Soviet equipment captured during various campaigns. In recent history, only the German Wehrmacht has paralleled the Israeli in this; no other army has captured so much equipment that they can afford to put it into service, maintain it and supply it with the right sort of ammunition.

Brigade HQ

Supplies, fuel, rations

4 SP guns and
1 bulldozer each

Heavy
machine guns

Repair workshop

Signal squadron

Mortars

4 APCs each

3 tanks each

20 tanks and APCs

Armored might Israeli M60 tanks move through the Sinai in 1975. The swirl of dust around the rear sprocket indicates the extreme conditions faced by armor in this part of the world and shows why the Israelis have firm views on what equipment is suitable for their use. The structure and equipment of a typical post-1973 Israeli armored brigade is shown **(bottom left)**

Uzi submachine gun, caliber 9mm, length (butt folded) 470mm (butt open) 650mm, weight 3.5kg (empty), magazine capacity 25/32 rounds, muzzle velocity 400 meters/second, rate of fire 600rpm, effective range 200 meters.

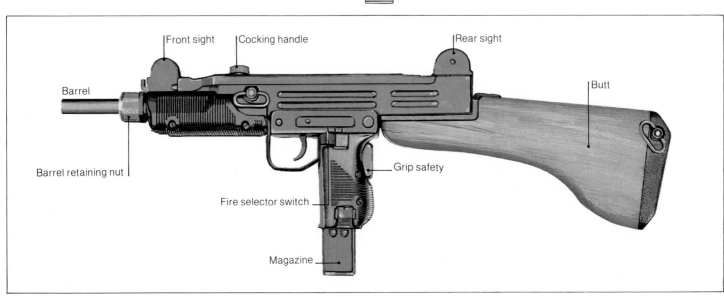

Front sight   Cocking handle   Rear sight

Barrel   Butt

Barrel retaining nut

Grip safety

Fire selector switch

Magazine

The Uzi in use Israeli women military police parade through Haifa, carrying their Uzi submachine guns **(left)**; an Israeli soldier, armed with an Uzi, gives chase to an Arab demonstrator **(right)**. The Uzi is an extremely handy weapon; it can be fired one-handed, if necessary.

Infantry Weapons

One of the legacies of the 1948 war was the realisation that a good submachine gun was a necessity. The wartime Sten gun was a remarkable enough weapon in its own way, but it left a great deal to be desired in its reliability, so in 1949 Lieutenant Uziel Gal began designing an improved model. He had previously studied a number of existing designs — notably the Czechoslovakian Models 24 and 26 — from which he took the idea of using a 'telescoped' bolt. The principle of this is that the front section of the bolt is hollow, and surrounds the barrel at the moment of firing; this allows the weapon to be much shorter while retaining a bolt mass sufficient to keep the rate of fire down to a level which permits good control of the gun during automatic firing. The resulting submachine gun, the Uzi, was introduced into Israeli service in the early 1950s and has since been widely exported and manufactured under license in other countries. It is undoubtedly one of the best designs of its class to appear in the past 40 years.

The Uzi is largely made from welded steel pressings, a method of manufacture which reduces cost and also enables machine shops with simple equipment to manufacture the weapon. The body is prominently grooved, which adds strength and stiffness to the pressings and also provides channels through which dust and sand can escape from the action in adverse conditions. Its reliability in desert warfare is a by-word. The telescoped bolt construction makes it possible to fit the magazine into the pistol grip; this, at the time of the Uzi's introduction, was unusual. It is a useful practical feature too, since, when changing magazines in the dark, it is merely necessary to bring the hand holding the magazine towards the hand holding the grip. This is an instinctive move which never fails. Trying to find a distantly-located magazine housing is another story altogether.

The standard magazine holds 32 rounds. A special clip is used to clamp two magazines together in an 'L' shape, one magazine entering the housing whilst the other points forward beneath the barrel. The additional weight of the second magazine helps to keep the muzzle down during automatic fire, while changing magazines is simply a matter of releasing the empty one, turning the combination so that the loaded one is vertical, and then inserting it into the pistol grip.

Israeli Military Industries, the company which makes the Uzi, have recently introduced the Mini-Uzi, a scaled-down version which is 110mm shorter than the standard model and correspondingly lighter. It has a folding wire stock (instead of the wooden or folding pressed-steel stock of the

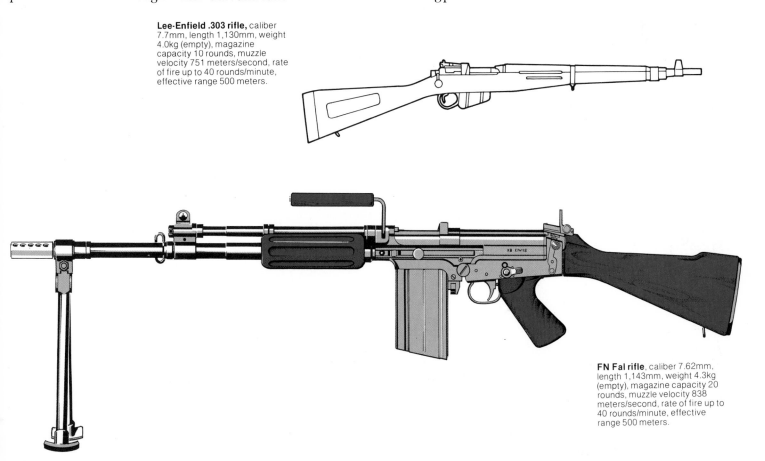

Lee-Enfield .303 rifle, caliber 7.7mm, length 1,130mm, weight 4.0kg (empty), magazine capacity 10 rounds, muzzle velocity 751 meters/second, rate of fire up to 40 rounds/minute, effective range 500 meters.

FN Fal rifle, caliber 7.62mm, length 1,143mm, weight 4.3kg (empty), magazine capacity 20 rounds, muzzle velocity 838 meters/second, rate of fire up to 40 rounds/minute, effective range 500 meters.

Accuracy in action Israeli troops use a 106mm recoilless rifle during the 1967 campaign. The ranging machine gun can be seen above the barrel; the rifle is aimed according to where the machine gun strikes, both being aligned together.

On the alert A signaller with his pack radio and Galil rifle outside the Beirut Museum **(right)**. Note how two magazines are taped together to allow a quick change in a fire fight. The infantryman **(far right)** is checking vehicle documents at a road block outside Hebron. He is armed with an M16A1 rifle.

full-sized Uzi) and is provided with special short 20- or 25-shot magazines, though the standard 32-shot magazine will still fit if required. The Mini-Uzi came into production only recently so that there is, as yet, no indication of its military adoption by any country, but it is anticipated that it will probably go into service with Israeli armored troops, and it will undoubtedly be exported.

The rifles used in the 1948 war were a heterogeneous collection of bolt-action weapons, largely a mixture of ex-British Lee-Enfields and ex-German Mausers. In the 1950s, these were scrapped and the Belgian FAL semi-automatic rifle in its 7.62mm NATO caliber version was universally adopted. During the Six-Day War of 1967, however, the Israeli Army acquired some American Armalite rifles firing the 5.56mm cartridge and, after several tests, it decided to re-equip with a 5.56mm rifle.

The 5.56mm caliber has several logistical advantages. The cartridge is smaller and lighter, so more can be carried or stored in a given space, the soldier carries less weight for his prescribed ammunition load, and the rifle itself can be lighter and more compact. All of these features are particularly attractive to an army fighting in desert conditions. Designs were requested, and several were put forward by various manufacturers, but after a series of trials the field was narrowed down to a handful of designs — the American Colt-Armalite M16A1; the American Stoner 63; the New Uzi design by Uziel Gal; the Soviet Kalashnikov AK47; and the Galil designed by Yaakov Lior and Israel Galili. Trial firings took place in desert conditions, special emphasis being laid upon the reliability of the weapons when faced with dust and sand. Of the weapons on the short list, it was eventually decided that the Galil

came closest to the stringent requirements which the Israeli Army had laid down, and its designers won the Annual Defence Award. Further development work went on in order to make slight improvements, and eventually, in 1972, the weapon was approved for manufacture and issue. Since then it has been closely studied in many other countries, and at least one foreign army (Sweden) appears likely to adopt a slightly modified version.

The Galil was designed to fill the roles of the rifle, the submachine gun and the squad light machine gun. In addition it can be used to fire anti-tank and anti-personnel grenades. It comes in various forms — a standard rifle, a heavy-barrelled rifle with a bipod for use as the squad automatic, a short-barrelled assault rifle and an even shorter version for use as a submachine gun. A 35 round magazine is used in the rifle role and a 50-round one in the machine gun role. The body of the rifle is made from steel pressings, and the mechanism is gas-operated, using a gas piston and bolt system closely modelled on the Soviet AK47 design. The sights allow aimed fire up to 500 metres, and luminous night sights are fitted as standard. Evidence of the practical aspects of the design are to be seen in the bipod, which doubles as a wire-cutter, and in the fact that a bottle-opener is incorporated, so as to stop soldiers damaging the magazines by using them to remove beer-bottle tops!

In 1982 a 7.62mm caliber Galil was announced. It is possible that this may be used in the light machine gun role by the Israeli forces, but it seems more likely that is has been designed as an export venture, to satisfy those armies who like the Galil but who are reluctant to accept the 5.56mm caliber.

Mortars
The Israeli infantry use mortars to good effect. All equipment is of local manufacture, though of basically foreign design. The infantry section mortar is a 52mm model made by Israeli Military Industries. It is simply a copy of the British 2in model, as are its bombs. Weighing under 8kg complete, the mortar can easily be operated by one man and throws a 920gm bomb to about 450 meters. It has no sight; its firer merely aligns a white line painted down the axis of the barrel with his target and elevates the barrel by experience and judgement. In spite of this apparent drawback, a trained soldier can produce rapid fire of surprising accuracy.

The larger mortars are made by Soltam, an Israeli company closely linked to the Tampella company of Finland and whose mortars are based on Tampella designs. The 60mm mortar is the standard light mortar, which is gradually replacing the 52mm model; it is rather more elegant

Comparisons The Colt-Armalite M16A1 and the Soviet Kalashnikov **(above and below right)** were both found to be inferior to the Galil by the Israelis.

Front sight

Rear sight

Handguard

Magazine

Magazine release

Fire selector switch (repetition, single shot, safe)

Standard equipment The Israeli-designed Galil is an extremely versatile infantry weapon, fulfilling the roles of rifle, submachine gun and squad light machine gun in its various forms. It can also fire anti-tank and anti-personnel grenades.

Supporting fire A battery of
120mm Soltam mortars in
action outside El Arish
during the 1967 campaign.

than the 52mm weapon. In its standard form, it has a circular baseplate and a bipod, together with a simple optical sight, and can fire a 1.7kg bomb to a range of 2,500 meters. A lighter version, without baseplate, bipod or directional sight, is called the Commando model. It is aimed through the use of the same white line as on the 52mm model but its elevation is controlled by a simple adjustable spirit level on the side. The weapon has a much shorter barrel than its 60mm counterpart and fires the same bomb to just under 1,000 meters. Finally there is the Long Range version, with a longer and heavier barrel which has a maximum range of 4,000 meters.

The company mortar is the 81mm, which comes in four versions — standard, long range, short barrel and split barrel. The standard version is a conventional enough design, with circular baseplate and bipod, firing a 3.9kg bomb to 4,700 meters. The long range model has a heavier and longer barrel and fires a 4.6kg bomb to 6,500 meters. The short barrel model fires the 3.9kg bomb to 4,000 meters. The split barrel version has the same performance as the standard model but the barrel is in two halves for ease of man-pack carriage or loading into small vehicles; the halves are joined by a screwed collar to produce a full-length barrel when the mortar is assembled.

The battalion mortar is the 120mm design,

M109 howitzer, caliber 155mm, shell weight 42.9kg, maximum muzzle velocity 562 meters/second, maximum range 14,600 meters, rate of fire 3 rounds per minute (short periods) 1 round per minute (sustained fire), ammunition carried 28 rounds. Vehicle weight 2,3750kg, length 6.25m, engine V-8 Detroit Diesel (405hp), road speed 56km/hr.

which is sufficiently light to allow it to be carried by animal pack, in light vehicles, or by its three-man crew. It fires a 12.9kg bomb to a maximum range of 7,200 meters. Its normal method of transport is on a light two-wheeled carriage, on to which the barrel, bipod and baseplate all fit very neatly.

The 81mm and 120mm mortars have been adapted on to a variety of self-propelled mountings in order to give additional mobility to the infantry support. Such modifications entail a change to the bipod and a new baseplate; with these, the mortars can be mounted into armoured personnel carriers, firing out through the roof hatch over the rear of the vehicle. The 81mm mortar can also be mounted in, and fired from, the M2A1 half-track scout vehicle. In all cases, the crew carry the normal bipod and baseplate on the vehicle, so that the mortar can be dismounted and fired from the ground in the normal way.

Artillery

After initially relying on a variety of war-surplus artillery pieces, the Israeli army standardized upon the American range of calibers and adopted American equipment in the 1950s, since these weapons were easily acquired and ammunition for them was available from several manufacturers. The 105mm M101 howitzer is the standard light support weapon as a result. This is an elderly design, having been first adopted by the US Army before the Second World War, but it has the advantage of being robust, simple, relatively esily to repair, while its spare parts are available from several sourcs. It fires a 15kg shell to a range of 11,200 meters, and the ammunition range covers high explosive, phosphorus smoke, illuminating, and shaped-charge anti-tank shells.

The drawback to the 105mm M101 is the date of its design; this means that by modern standards the shell is insufficiently lethal, and the range is too short, particularly in comparison with more modern Soviet weapons, in which the length of the range has always been one of the prime design factors. Over the past two decades, most armies have moved to a 155mm howitzer for 'general support' purposes; such a gun is capable of firing a shell weighing about 45kg to a range of about 20,000 meters. It can be readily appreciated that, firstly, this type of weapon can deliver a much more powerful and lethal shell than its 105mm counterpart, and, secondly, it can cover a far greater area. Assuming a gun to have an arc of fire of 60°, the 105mm with a range of 11,200 meters will command an area of 65 square kilometers, while a 155mm howitzer with a range of 18,100 meters will command an area of 171 square kilometers.

Another important post war artillery development has been the increasing adoption of self-propelled guns and howitzers, mounted on motorised tracked chassis so that they can drive rapidly into and out of position and move rapidly across country. This cross-country ability is particularly useful in a desert environment since the nature of the terrain favors tracked vehicles over wheeled ones. As a result a tracked self-propelled weapon can move more reliably than can a conventional gun towed by a wheeled vehicle. The Israeli Army began examining the virtues of self-propelled artillery in the 1950s and experimented with a number of local designs, grafting various types of artillery piece on to chassis adapted from existing and obsolescent tanks, such as the war-time Sherman. A further factor is the Israeli tendency to fast-moving motorized warfare, which favors the employment of self-propelled guns, and another is the fact that the Israeli forces operate from interior lines. This is the classic term which applies to any country surrounded by enemies, and signifies the ability to switch its defensive forces rapidly from one frontier to another to counter aggression. The attacker, on the other hand, in attempting to encircle the country, must rely upon extended exterior lines of communication, perhaps across captured territory, vulnerable to attack, difficult to coordinate and slow to respond. In such a situation the ability to move self-propelled guns at speed is a considerable advantage to the defender.

Mobile support A 120mm mortar mounted in a half-tracked carrier, in use during the 1973 war. The plastic bags around the bomb tails are to protect the propelling cartridges, which are clipped around the tail.

Two crewmen support the tray. Once the shell is in the chamber, all three use the rammer staff to ram the shell into the rifling

Crew chief receives orders from fire direction center

One crewman pushes the shell into the chamber from the loading tray

Open fire The four-man firing crew load an SP 155mm howitzer **(left)**. The howitzer has just fired **(below)** and, as the dust settles, the crew dash forward to open the breech and reload.

As a result of these arguments the Israelis have adopted several self-propelled weapons, largely of American design and manufacture since these have been readily available under export agreements from the USA. Among the first was the 155mm self-propelled howitzer M109, a weapon widely used throughout NATO and many other countries. The M109 has a welded aluminum armor hull carried on tracks, with a similiar armored turret as a mounting for the 155mm howitzer. The howitzer is fitted with a muzzle brake to reduce the recoil stresses on the mounting, and with a fume extractor to remove the poisonous products of the cartridge explosion from the barrel before the breech is opened, so keeping fumes out of the turret during firing. The turret will traverse full circle and the gun can be elevated to a maximum of 75°. The Americans have a wide variety of ammunition available, but, as far as is known, the Israeli artillery uses only high explosive, illuminating and white phosphorus smoke projectiles.

The original M109 had a maximum range of 14,600 meters, which was not particularly impressive for the size of the equipment. It was therefore improved in the early 1970s by fitting a new, longer, barrel which extended the maximum range to 18,000 meters. At the same time some mechanical improvements to the elevation and traverse mechanisms were made and the torsion-bar suspension of the track wheels was improved. In Israeli service the modified weapons are designated M109AL. They also have additional stowage racks on the hull and turret sides to enable a greater quantity of ammunition to be carried on the vehicle.

When the 155mm caliber was adopted, Israel again looked to Soltam. The company developed a suitable 155mm howitzer barrel and then built it on to a modified Sherman M4A3E8 tank chassis. The basic Sherman had the turret removed and the upper hull cut away, and the sides of the hull were made into a vertical-walled compartment with the howitzer mounted so as to fire over the front of the vehicle. The engine was removed and replaced by a modern Cummins diesel motor. Doors in the side armor allow entrance and exit for the gun crew, and 60 rounds of ammunition can be carried inside the armor. The howitzer has a maximum range of 21,000 meters and fires the same projectiles and cartridges as the American M109 series weapons. Known as the L-33, this Soltam equipment entered service in 1973 and was used for the first time in the 1973 war.

In 1981, Soltam announced a totally new design of self-propelled 155mm howitzer, designated M72. This has been developed as a private venture — not to meet an Israeli army specification. It is simply a self-contained turreted howitzer, which can replace the standard turret in virtually any current main battle tank. Thus, an army with spare Centurion or M48 tanks, for example, could remove the turrets, make some minor modifications to the interior of the hull to provide ammunition racks, and then drop the Soltam turret unit into the hulls to make self-propelled howitzers. The M72 howitzer fires standard 155mm shells and charges and can attain a maximum range of 20,500 meters. There is an alternative, longer, barrel which fits the same turret and which will permit a maximum range of 23,500 meters. So far, there has been no announcement of the official adoption of this weapon by the Israelis.

In order to achieve the greatest possible range with current conventional artillery the Israelis

Ready for action A 175mm gun is readied for action, the bore being swabbed out and the and the ammunition detail preparing the cartridge bags **(left)**. Another 175mm takes up position on the Golan Heights **(below)**. The support vehicle, in front of the gun, carries some of the gun crew, ammunition, equipment and bedding.

purchased a number (about 60) of 174mm M107 self-propelled guns from the USA. This weapon was developed by the Americans as part of an air-transportable family of self-propelled vehicles, so the chassis is remarkably light for its role; this reduction in size and weight was made possible by development of a highly efficient hydraulic locking system which, applied to the suspension, and allied with a recoil spade lowered at the rear of the chassis, keeps the weapon stable when firing. The gun is mounted in the open, on top of the chassis, there being no armor or other protection for the crew when in action.

The 175mm gun fires a shell weighing 67kg to a maximum range of 32,700 meters; with the standard 60° arc of fire it can command an area of 560 square kilometres. The gun can traverse 30° to left and right on its mounting, and can elevate to a maximum of 65°. There is a powered loader/rammer assembly which lifts the shell from the ground alongside the gun, places it on the loading tray and rams it into the chamber.

However, the 175mm gun has had a somewhat mixed history; it was widely adopted throughout NATO but several armies suffered accidents which were found to be due to ammunition faults. These were eventually corrected, as were various defects in the chassis electrical system, the engine cooling system and the loader/rammer hydraulics. It is possible that the Israeli Army suffered similar problems, though there is no official information to back up this theory. In NATO service the 175mm gun is now being phased out, since its long-range performance can now be duplicated by tactical missiles and by a new generation of improved 155mm weapons, while in the US the guns have been removed from their chassis and replaced with 203mm howitzers. Whether the Israelis will follow suit remains to be seen, but it is probable that they will retain the guns as they are, since their maximum range is of considerable value in the Israeli military situation.

The 203mm howitzer mentioned above is also used by the Israeli Army. This is a 'partner piece' to the 175mm gun insofar as it is mounted on the same chassis (which is why the Americans have substituted it for the 175mm gun). The howitzer, though, is an elderly design, having been developed as a towed weapon in the USA in the 1930s and used throughout the Second World War. It fires a shell weighing 92.5kg to a maximum range of 16,800 meters. This is not particularly impressive by modern standards and the Americans therefore have developed two improved versions, the M110A1 and the M110A2. The M110A1 has a longer barrel and can reach a range of 21,300 meters, while the latter has a muzzle brake which allows the firing of a more powerful propelling charge to reach to 29,100 meters. The Israeli Army purchased 48 M110 203mm howitzers, but how many of these have since been converted to M110A1 standard is not known.

The advantages of self-propulsion also apply to the 105mm weapons. The Israeli Army employs 130 American-built M108 SP 105mm weapons, and probably still has a number of M7, an earlier design of which it once had some 120 in service. The M7 dates from 1942 and was a modified M3 tank chassis mounting the standard 105mm field howitzer. It was widely used by the British and American armies and the Israel M7s were purchased in the postwar years from surplus stocks. The principal drawback to the M7 is that the crew compartment is open topped, leaving men and ammunition vulnerable to air attack. The M108 version, developed in the 1960s, is turretted to give the crew full protection. It uses aluminium armor for hull and turret, and the gun is fitted with a fume extractor. Its performance is identical with that of the towed 105mm howitzer, firing a 15kg shell to 11,200 meters range.

As has been mentioned already, the various Arab-Israeli wars have furnished the Israeli Army with a vast amount of booty in the form of captured guns and equipment. From this haul the artillery has benefitted by some 450 Soviet guns of various calibers. The principal stocks are of the 122mm M1938 howitzer; the 122mm D-30 howitzer; and the 130mm M46 gun.

As the title implies, the 122mm M1938 howitzer is an elderly weapon. It appears to have been utilized principally for training, though, of course, it could be used in combat if the need arose. It is a conventional split-trail weapon, firing a 22kg shell to a range of 11,800 meters.

The 122mm D-30 howitzer is the weapon which the Soviets introduced in the early 1960s to replace the M1938 in their own army, and it was subsequently exported to several Middle Eastern countries. It is said to have been designed by the F F Petrov Bureau of Artillery Design at Sverdlovsk, but it is similar in many design points to a design developed by Skoda of Czechoslovakia for the German Army in 1943. The gun sits on a three-legged carriage when in action, its wheels raised from the ground, so that it can be rapidly traversed through 360°. It can elevate to 70° and fires a 21.7kg shell to a maximum range of 15,400 meters. For transportation, the carriage legs are folded together and the wheels lowered; the barrel is clamped to the central carriage leg, and a towing eye, attached to the muzzle, connected to the towing vehicle.

The 130mm M46 gun was developed by the Soviets in the early 1950s, and rapidly become their standard divisional artillery weapon. It fires a 33.4kg shell to a range of 27,150 meters with phenomenal accuracy, and, after the Soviet Ar-

my had been outfitted, it was exported widely to many African and Far Eastern countries. Israel captured a large number from Egypt, Iraq and Syria and put them into service. In its original form, the 130mm uses a two-wheeled carriage with split trail. When being towed, the original design called for the very long barrel to be disconnected from its recoil system and pulled back until the breech ring is secured about half-way along the trail; this reduced the barrel overhang and cut down the vibration (which placed stress on the elevating gears). This system, whilst satisfactory in saving the mechanisms from premature wear and tear, means that the weapon is slow to get into and out of action, and the Israeli Army has therefore made some modifications. The wheels have been removed and replaced by a four-wheeled bogie carried on a walking-beam suspension; this gives a more stable ride to the carriage, and, together with a redesigned elevation gearbox, allows the weapon to be towed without retracting the gun barrel.

Armored Vehicles

In the 1950s Israel purchased most of its armored vehicles from France or Britain; from the former it acquired a number of modified Sherman tanks and French-built AMX-13 light tanks, and from the latter a number of Centurion main battle tanks. Shortly before the 1967 war the British also

Captured booty A range of the vast amount of Soviet equipment the Israelis have destroyed or captured is shown here. The 122mm howitzer model 1938 **(right)** was one of many Egyptian guns wrecked by the Israelis in 1967. In the background is a 160mm Soviet mortar. Two small Israelis **(far right)** examine a 130mm Soviet gun, one exhibit in a collection of booty captured in the 1967 campaign. Behind them is an American 105mm Priest self-propelled howitzer.

Under new ownership
Jubilant Israeli troops pose around a Soviet 76mm gun, captured in the Sinai campaign of 1974. Many such weapons were still in working order and used against their former owners **(left)**. Israeli 130mm guns on the Golan Heights **(below)**; these are also captured weapons. The Israelis have adapted the gun-carriage of this model for greater efficiency.

New weapon A Merkava tank during exercises in early 1980. This was the first time the existence of the Merkava was officially confirmed — before this, it had been one of Israel's closely-guarded secrets.

provided two Chieftain tanks for appraisal, but after the war they declined to supply any more, though they continued to provide Centurions. A number of American-built M48 tanks were sold to Israel by West Germany, but Arab political pressure stopped the supply. Israel then turned to the USA, from which it was able to obtain M48 and M60 tanks. The present Israeli strength from outside resources is believed to be approximately 1,000 Centurions, 650 M48s, 810 M60s, and possibly 200 M47s.

These figures show for themselves that, if the Arabs were able to apply successful pressure to the USA, the supply of tanks would rapidly dry up. For this reason, the Israelis decided to proceed with the development of a tank of their own, which, though built in Israel, would, where possible, utilize existing components.

Traditionally, the tank is the coming-together of three battle demands — mobility, protection and fire-power — and the way these three are apportioned depend entirely on the individual preferences of the army which commissions the design. In the case of the Israelis, their experience in the 1967 war convinced them that, as far as battle tanks were concerned, armor for protection came first, firepower second, and mobility last,

and the designers set to work within this framework of priorities. Broad principles were discussed from 1967 onwards, but it was not until 1970 that a design team under General Israel Tal began detailed work, with a great deal of financial and technical assistance from the USA. In 1977 the project was revealed to the world by the announcement that the new tank, named Merkava (Chariot), was in prototype stage and that a first pre-production run of 40 vehicles was to be built. The first production tanks were delivered to the army in 1979, and by the end of 1982 it is understood that some 325 are now in service, with production continuing.

The hull of the Merkava is of cast armored steel, with a broad and well-sloped glacis plate at the front. The armor construction is quite unique; it is in two layers and between them is a space filled with diesel fuel. It is claimed that this form of construction gives protection against the shaped-charge warheads used in anti-tank guided missiles. The turret and fighting compartment are at the rear of the hull, another unusual feature since all other contemporary tank designs place the turret in the centre. The driver is seated in the left front of the hull, and the engine compartment is to his right; it is this forward placement of the

Into action Merkava tanks enter Beirut in August 1982 Their crews are ready for action, in their bullet-proof 'flak' jackets.

Merkava tank, combat weight 56,000kg, length 7.12m, width 3.70m, engine Continental V-12 diesel (900hp), gun 105mm, road speed, maximum range, armor all classified.

engine which permits the fighting compartment to be set to the rear, while it is further claimed that the mass of the engine acts as a protection against frontal attack. An armor-piercing projectile might penetrate the frontal armour, but, if so, it would lodge in the engine instead of entering the fighting compartment. The tank would, of course, be rendered immobile (if nothing worse) but at least the lives of the crew would be saved, and manpower is a precious commodity to the Israelis.

The engine is an American Continental diesel V-12 developing 900 horsepower, while the Allison transmission used is similar to that of the American M60 series of tanks. The turret is a welded structure and will accept either a 105mm or 120mm gun; at present the Merkava mounts a 105mm gun but it is undoubtedly intended to fit a 120mm in the future. The commander sits on the right side of the turret, with the gunner in front of and below him; the loader is on the other side of the turret. There are three hatches in the rear face of the hull; the one on the right gives access to a chemical warfare air filter, the one on the left to the vehicle's batteries, while the central hatch is a two-part door, opening up and down, giving access to the interior of the fighting compartment. When the Merkava was first announced and details of this door were given, it was widely assumed that the object was to permit fully-equipped infantrymen to be carried along into battle, but subsequent information indicates that the doorway is barely large enough for an infantryman to squeeze through in full fighting equipment, and that its primary function is to permit easy loading of ammunition, and possibly the transportation of wounded men. Up to four stretcher cases or nine walking wounded can be accommodated.

The 105mm rifled gun carried as main armament is manufactured in Israel but generally conforms to the British L7 design which has been adopted throughout the world. This permits British or American ammunition to be fired from it, though the Israelis now produce ammunition of their own, which they claim is superior to the American types. At least 65 rounds can be carried inside the tank, but this can be increased to 85 rounds if needed, while additional ammunition can be stacked in the rear door entry and on the floor of the fighting compartment at the price of some inconvenience.

The Merkava is fitted with an extremely sophisticated and modern fire control system based around a digital computer and aided by a laser rangefinder. The gunner lays his sight on to the target and presses a button; this 'fires' the laser rangefinder, and the range is fed into the computer. The computer also receives information on the tilt of the vehicle, the direction and strength

of the wind, the ambient temperature, the temperature of the propelling charge, the type of ammunition in use, and the barometric pressure. By integrating the gunlayer's tracking of the target, the computer calculates the target speed, works out the aiming correction required for that and for the ballistic conditions, and then displaces the sight cross-wire appropriately. This takes no more than a second or two; the gunner then relays the gun until the sight crosswire intersects the target, and fires with a high probability of a first-round hit. If required, the commander can take over control and fire the main armament without leaving his position.

An improved Mark 2 Merkava is currently under devlopment. This will have improved armor protection and an advanced hydro-pheumatic suspension system, which is being developed in the USA. The present Merkava uses a coil spring suspension and Centurion-type road-wheels. There is also a Mark 3 projected; as well as Mark 2 improvements, this will have a more powerful 1,200 horsepower engine and probably the 120mm gun.

Although the Merkava is one of the most up-to-date tanks of its kind, as yet it forms only a relatively small part of the Israeli armored strength. For some years to come, the force will still rely mainly upon the earlier models. These, though, are not quite in the same form as they were when they left the manufacturer's factories; combat experience has led to several improvements being grafted onto them, so that the Israeli Centurion, for example, is significantly different to anyone else's Centurion.

The Centurion first went into service with the Israeli Army in 1959. At first it was disliked. Compared to the Shermans they were then using, the Israelis found the Centurion a complicated and advanced machine. These initial misgivings died down, however, once it was realized what an efficient fighting weapon the tank was, but even then there were technical defects, which made themselves apparent in the harsh desert conditions. The Meteor engine gave the tank a poor power-to-weight ratio and was prodigal of fuel, while the cooling and air filtration systems gave constant trouble. By the late 1960s it was decided to replace the Meteor engine with the American engine which powered the M48 tank, while the original manual gearbox was replaced by an American automatic transmission. In order to shoe-horn this engine into the Centurion hull, some alteration was demanded. The result, known as the Upgraded Centurion, is easily recognised by its raised engine deck and prominent air filters.

The Centurion is armed with a 105mm gun, the original form of that used in the Merkava and firing the same ammunition. Although little infor-

To suit conditions An Israeli Centurion bustles at speed through the dust of the Negev **(above)**. To combat such conditions, the Israelis fitted new engines and transmissions to the tank. They also raised the engine deck and fitted special air filters — these can be seen behind the Centurion, photographed during maneouvers in May 1967 **(right)**.

mation has been released, it is likely that the fire control system is less sophisticated than that used on the Merkava, though it is possible that the Merkava system could be adapted to the Centurion's if desired.

The American M48 and M60 tanks are cousins under the skin and, when modifications and changes are taken into account, can be very difficult to tell apart. The M48 dates from the Korean War when in 1950, the USA found itself without a medium tank and responded by hurrying the M48 design into production — too hurriedly, as it turned out, since it was some years before the initial teething troubles were overcome and the tank became combat-reliable. In its basic form the M48 mounts a 90mm gun, has a crew of four men, and a 750 horsepower diesel engine.

The M60 tank was begun in 1956 with the intention of improving on the basic M48 design by

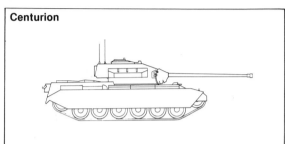

Centurion

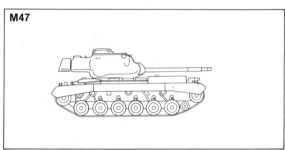

M47

M60

The Centurion **(above)** was one of the most successful tanks of its day. It achieved the distinction of being ordered both by Israel and its Arab neighbours.

Centurion cruiser tank, combat weight 51,820kg, length 7.79m, width 3.30m, engine Rolls-Royce Meteor V-12 (as originally supplied), gun 105mm, road speed 35km/hr, range 200km, armor 17-152mm.

Battle tank The M60, developed by the US Army, was bought by the Israelis in the adapted M60A1 version. This proved superior to Soviet equivalents supplied to the Arabs.

M48 medium tank, combat weight 47,173kg, length 6.88m, width 3.63m, engine Continental 1790-2A V-12 diesel, armament 90mm M41, road speed 48km/hr, range 465km, armor 12-120mm.

The fist of steel Armored superiority in machines, men and tactics has been one of the keys to Israeli success. A tank column **(below)** sweeps through the Sinai to show the flat, but, even on this exercise, the tanks' guns cover all points of the compass. M60s **(left)** move towards the Bek'aa Valley, M50 Shermans **(far left)**, re-equipped with French turrets and 75mm guns, lead a peaceful independence day parade and **(far right)** enter a liberated Jerusalem.

improving the armament, operational range and mobility and reducing the maintenance and servicing load. Slightly longer than the M48, its general appearance is similar but it carries a 105mm gun and is driven by an air-cooled 750 horsepower diesel. The fire control system was greatly improved, a laser rangefinder replacing the M48's optical rangefinder with a solid-state ballistic computer producing the data for the gunner.

Most of the Israeli M48s have been virtually turned into M60s by replacing the 90mm gun with the locally-manufactured 105mm weapon, adding the improved fire control system, and installing the air-cooled diesel engine. 650 M48s and 810 M60s had been delivered by the beginning of 1981. Since then a further order for 200 of the latest version of the M60 has been placed and deliveries are currently in progress.

In the early days of the Israeli armored force the principal battle tank was the Sherman, in many variant models and armed with a variety of guns. These were mostly brought up to improved standards by local modifications. Two of the most important of these were the M50, in which a new turret with a French 75mm gun was fitted, and the M51 which carried a specially-modified French 105mm gun. These were used with considerable success in the 1967 and 1973 wars, in the last of which they both successfully engaged the Soviet T-62s supplied to Syria and Egypt. By now, though, more modern tanks have replaced both models in first-line service. While a few gun Shermans may be left in training or reserve formations, the majority have had their guns removed and have been converted into various specialised forms. These include armored ambulances, artillery command and observation vehicles, mine-clearing tanks, bulldozer tanks and bridgelayers.

As with artillery, so with armored vehicles, since the strength of the Israeli army has been substantially augmented by Soviet tanks captured from the Egyptian and Syrian armies in the 1967 and 1973 conflicts. It is believed that some 400 T54/55s and 150 T62s are held in working order by the Israelis and have been assimilated into their armored forces.

The T54/55 series Soviet tanks are usually considered together, since the differences between them are relatively minor. The T54 appeared in 1949. It is a low-slung vehicle with a well-curved turret and a 100mm rifled gun, a 520 horsepower water-cooled diesel engine and an all-up weight of about 36 tonnes. In common with many early Soviet tank designs, the turret was simply a rotating structure above the hull; unlike Western tanks, it has no 'basket', the suspended floor upon which the crew stood so that, wherever the turret moved, they moved with it. In Soviet tanks of the period the loader had to walk around the hull

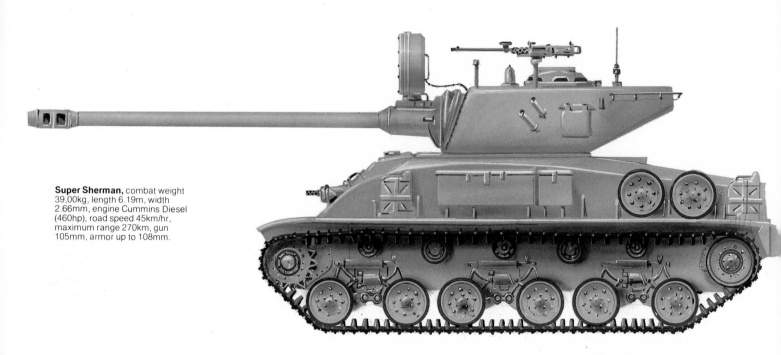

Super Sherman, combat weight 39,00kg, length 6.19m, width 2.66mm, engine Cummins Diesel (460hp), road speed 45km/hr, maximum range 270km, gun 105mm, armor up to 108mm.

floor as the turret turned. In the T55, however, the problem was solved in a most complex manner by arranging for a section of the hull floor to rotate in sympathy with the turret; there was also an increase in engine power to 580 horsepower, the gun was stabilised for elevation and traverse, and there was more room for ammunition inside the hull.

After capture by the Israelis, several (though not all) of these T54/55 series tanks have been extensively modified. The 100mm Soviet gun has been discarded and replaced by a 105mm gun, the engine has been replaced by an American diesel, air-conditioning fitted, the fire control system and sights vastly improved, and the co-axial and anti-aircraft machine guns replaced by Western designs firing ammunition compatible with the rest of the Israeli forces. Many have also had night vision equipment incorporated in their sighting and observation fittings. With all these changes the nomenclature has been changed to TI-67.

The T62 was developed from the T54/55 series and first appeared in public in 1965. While similar in general appearance to the T54/55, it is longer and wider, has the roadwheels differently spaced, and has a longer and thicker gun barrel with a prominent fume extractor close to the muzzle. Its principal improvement is its gun, which is a smooth-bored 115mm weapon of advanced design; in fact this turned out to be somewhat disappointing, proving to be less accurate and to have a slower rate of fire than the 100mm. In addition, the highly ingenious automatic spent-case ejection system, which removed the case from the gun breech and propelled it through a sprung

hatch in the rear of the turret, also proved a problem. In practice it was found that the ejector frequently missed the trapdoor, resulting in a large, hot brass case bouncing around inside the turret. In the war of 1973 both Egypt and Syria put these tanks into action and they proved to be no match for the Israelis.

So far as is known, the Israeli T62s have had no major modifications carried out on them, probably because any changes would not be cost-effective. Doubtless the automatic case ejection gear has been scrapped and the fire control system improved, but the gun is basically a poor design with a slow rate of fire and it is probably that the Israelis are using these as training tanks, rather than relying upon them as first-line fighting vehicles.

Rockets and Missiles
The Israeli Army has some 218 Lance battlefield support missiles which it purchased from the USA. These are organized into three battalions, each with nine M752 launch vehicles. The Lance is a liquid-fuelled rocket with inertial guidance, mid-course corrections being supplied by a ground control station which makes constant and precise measurements of the missile's trajectory. It has a speed of Mach 3, due to the use of pre-packed, storable liquid propellant, and a range of about 120 kilometers with a very high degree of accuracy. The US Army has a nuclear warhead, but the Israeli missiles are provided only with the M251 cluster fragmentation warhead. This contains 836 individual bomblets, which are dispersed over the target and, on impact, distribute their

Fortunes of war An Egyptian T-54 **(right)** lies abandoned after a disabling shot in the engine compartment. The tank's smoothly rounded turret was designed to make attacking shells ricochet, but there is still a shot trap, where the turret overhangs the hull. The Israeli M48A2, with 90mm gun, is on the Jerusalem to Amman road **(far right)**. The M48 was later upgraded with a 105mm gun.

T54

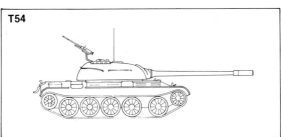

T-54 (Egyptian), combat weight 36,000kg, length 6.45m, width 3.27m, engine V-12 diesel (520hp), road speed 48km/hr, maximum range 400km, gun 100m, armor up to 203mm.

T-62 (Syrian), combat weight 40,000kg, length 6.3m, width 3.30m, engine V-12 diesel (580hp), road speed 50km/hr, maximum range 450km, gun 115mm, armor up to 242mm.

Firing the Lance The photographs show the three stages in firing the Lance battlefield support missile. In the first, the missile is seen on its mobile launcher; the cab is being dismantled so as not to be wrecked by the launch blast. The rear view shows the rocket jet; the crew's anti-gas respirators are part of a mock chemical warfare alert. Finally, Lance fires. The main motor propels the missile upwards, with subsidiary motors in the mid-body spinning it slowly to aid its accuracy.

fragments over an area of some 900 meters in diameter. They cause damage through a combination of blast and splinters.

Very little has been revealed about a locally manufactured missile, the Ze'ev (Wolf), which was apparently used with success in the 1973 war, though its existence was not officially revealed until some six months later. It is understood that Ze'ev is a short-range battlefield support missile, available in two very different versions. The first carries a 170kg warhed and has a range of about 1,000 meters; the second has a 70kg warhead and can reach to 4,000 metres. The missiles are said to be fired from a frame-type launcher, and are reported to be not very accurate, but devastating against massed troops and vehicles. From this brief description it would appear that both Ze'ev variants should be defined more properly as rockets rather than missiles, since the use of the latter term implies the existence of some sort of guidance or control system.

The Israelis had little to do with rockets until they captured large numbers of Soviet rocket launchers from Egypt and Syria in 1967. One particular model, the Soviet BM-24, fell into their hands in such quantities that it wa thought worthwhile putting them into Israeli service, and suitable rockets for the launchers are now manufactured locally. The BM-24 rocket is 240mm in diameter, has a solid-propellant motor at the rear, and carries a warhead containing 18kg of high explosive. The whole rocket weighs 110kg when loaded and has a maximum range of 10,700 meters.

The launcher is a frame unit mounted on a 6x6 truck, capable of holding 12 rockets and firing them in a 'ripple', in which the entire loading is shot off in about three seconds. There is a slight interval between each ignition so that the next rocket to be fired is not deflected by the blast of the previous shot. The rockets are spun during flight by having the efflux nozzles suitably inclined; this gives them a reasonable degree of accuracy, the probable error being in the region of one per cent of the range. Soviet use of such rockets goes back to the Second World War.

Perhaps inspired by these Soviet models, recent information is that the Israelis have now developed a rocket system of their own — the MAR (Medium Artillery Rocket) 290. This is thought to have been originally developed to the order of an anonymous NATO country, and it has since been taken into Israeli service. From the few details that have been released, the weapon appears to be a solid-fuel rocket of 290mm diameter, launched from a frame launcher mounted on a tank chassis, and with a probable range of 20 kilometers.

As might be imagined, the Israelis see their chief threat coming from enemy armored formations, and, indeed, the Israelis probably know more than any other fighting force about the art of tank warfare as it exists today. Using tanks to kill tanks is a wasteful process, however; moreover, there is no guarantee that a defensive tank will be in the right place at the right time to deal with an invader. For this reason Israeli weapon designers have concentrated for some years on developing lightweight anti-tank weapons for use by the infantry, while the Israelis also have purchased a number of these from time to time.

The basic Israeli anti-tank weapon is the American 106mm recoilless gun, which fires a fin-stabilised shaped-charge shell capable of penetrating over 200mm of armor. Like most such weapons it has a considerable maximum range — 7,700 meters — but its practical range against tanks is considered to be only 1,000 meters due to the relatively slow flight of the shell and the difficulty of aiming-off for target movement. Ranging is carried out by a spotting rifle mounted on top of the barrel; this is a converted .50 machine gun firing a special explosive bullet which is ballistically matched to the gun's shell. The gunner takes aim and fires the spotting rifle. If he hits the target, he then fires the main gun, assured that his aim is correct; if he misses with the spotting shot, then he re-aims and repeats until he has a strike on target. The principal drawback of the recoilless gun lies in its method of operation; the cartridge case is constructed to allow a major part of the propellant gases to be ejected to the rear to balance the recoil thrust set

No longer the enemy
Captured Soviet BM24 mobile battlefield rocket launchers now form an important part of Israel's missile arsenal. The Israelis manufacture their own ammunition and have improved the original Soviet design. A battery of BM24 rockets **(left)** in a firing position. Reversing off the track means that the rockets will throw up less dust and debris when launched. BM24 launchers are seen on the move **(below)** and **(bottom)** in action. Note how the vehicles are shrouded in canvas, partly for camouflage and partly to protect them against blast as the rockets accelerate.

up by the departing projectile. This rearward flame and blast is impossible to conceal, so, once the recoilless gun has fired, its position is exposed.

The various types of small missile in Israeli service are more sophisticated. They use the American TOW and Dragon, the French SS-11, the German Cobra, and the Soviet Sagger (captured from Egypt). All these work in a similar fashion, though some are more advanced than others. In their basic form they consist of a rocket-propelled warhead, which contains an efficient shaped charge capable of penetrating 300mm of armor. This is launched from a ground mounting and thereafter controlled in flight so as to be steered to the target by the firer. As the missile

Survivor Though modern anti-aircraft missiles have taken ove many of its functions, the Bofors 40mm anti-aircraft gun **(below)** is still a useful defensive weapon.

Snapper captured Three Israeli soldiers **(above)** examine a Soviet Snapper missile launcher, captured during the 1967 Sinai campaign. Snapper was the first wire-guided anti-tank missile to be produced by the Soviet bloc. In the background is another captured missile, the Soviet SA-2 Guideline anti-aircraft missile.

flies through the air, so it unwinds wire from an interior spool. One end of the wire is attached to the firing control unit and carries electronic signals from the controller to the flight surfaces of the missile.

The earliest of these anti-tank missiles are the SS-11 and the Cobra, both being 'first-generation' missiles. This means it is necesary for the operator to track the missile and, with a joystick control, actually steer it to impact with the target. The Soviet Sagger employs the same system, and it was their successful experience in countering Sagger in 1973 that led the Isrealis to see its defects. Put simply, the operator must give his full attention to the missile during its flight, and must have a very sensitive touch on the controls. As the Israelis discovered, a burst of machine gun fire directed at the operator is usually enough to take his mind off his job and so to lose control of the missile.

The American TOW and Dragon, however, are second-generation missiles. They operate in much the same way, but control is semi-automatic from the sighting system. The tail of the missile carries an infra-red flare, and the missile is pre-programmed to fly into the sight line after it is launched. The operator merely has to keep his sight aligned with the target; he takes no notice of the missile. As the missile flies, so the

flare is seen in the sight and is sensed by an infrared detector which forms part of the sight array. This is capable of sensing the displacement of the flare from the centerline of the sight. Having determined this, a computer calculates the correction necessary to move the missile into the sight's center. Commands are sent down the wire to the missile steering it into the sight line. In practice there is a slight over-correction, so that the sight now has a fresh calculation to perform and fresh commands to send, but the misalignment is rapidly cancelled out to ensure the missile finally sits in the sight axis. Provided the operator is efficient enough to keep the sight pointed at the target, a hit is almost inevitable.

As with other weapons, the Israelis felt that reliance on foreign sources of supply was unsatisfactory, particularly since anti-tank missiles are weapons likely to be needed in some numbers. For this reason Israeli Military Industries have developed their own anti-tank weapon, called Picket. Since this is unguided, it is a good deal less expensive than the TOW and Dragon, but it uses a novel form of control to make it extremely accurate. The rocket was devised in response to the Israeli tactical doctrine that the infantryman needed a light, powerful and accurate weapon with which he could engage armored personnel carriers. If the APCs

Launching a TOW This 18kg missile flies at over 1,000 km/hr to reach targets up to 3,750m away, guided by signals along the wire which trails behind it. The shaped charge warhead is capable of penetrating any tank in the world.

The anatomy of TOW Developed by the USA, TOW uses its simple, but effective, wire guidance system to deal with moving or stationary targets.

TOW United States

(Tube-launched, Optically-tracked, Wire-guided anti-tank missile). Solid fuelled two-stage motor. Range up to 13,000 feet. Launch weight 40 lbs.

TOW's operator **(1)** tracks the target by eye through his sight and launches the missile. The telescopic sight's infra-red sensor keeps track of the missile and feeds information into a computer. The stabilizing fins fold out **(2)** and the wires unwind from the back to carry any guidance instructions. The computer is alerted to any deviations in flight path, corrects these and steers the missile until it reaches its target **(3)**.

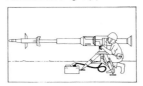

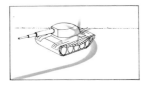

Infra-red guidance The US Redeye anti-aircraft missile is Israel's main lightweight battlefield defence, as it can be fired by a single infantryman **(right)**. It locks on to its target by detecting the infra-red emissions from engine and jet pipe.

Close support The Israelis have mounted 160mm Tampella mortars in redundant tank chassis **(below)**, so creating a formidable close-support bombardment weapon, which can be moved rapidly from place to place.

can be attacked successfully, then the armored element of a combined force is stripped of its infantry protection and can be dealt with more easily. Though designed with APCs in mind, Picket however, appears to be powerful enough to deal with any main battle tank likely to be found in the vicinity of Israel in the forseeable future.

Picket consists of a short launch tube, with sight and firing grips, containing a rocket with shaped charge warhead. The rocket also contains a gyroscopic control unit, a guidance package and a thrust vectoring system, which can steer the rocket by means of four tabs in the rocket efflux. The operator takes aim at the target and fires; an ejection motor launches the rocket and imparts stabilising spin to it. On leaving the muzzle three fins spring out, and the ejection motor is discarded. After a short free flight, the main motor lights and the rocket now accelerates down-range at supersonic speed. The gyroscope senses any deviation from a perfectly straight and flat course and, by means of the guidance package, moves the four thrust vectoring tabs to keep the course of the rocket flat and straight. Because of this flat trajectory, range estimation is not as important as usual, and, because of the very fast flight, aim-off for moving targets is minimal. Once the rocket has been fired the operator throws the launcher away and gets another one. The entire package weights only 6kg and has a maximum range of 500 meters.

Anti-Aircraft Defense

The Israelis see the principal air defense requirement as being for their field forces, since their potential enemies have very little strategic bombing capability and put all their aerial effort into strafing attacks on the troops in the field. Therefore the air defence is principally built around light and fast-firing guns, while the field troops are provided with lightweight guided anti-aircraft missiles fired from the shoulder.

The field air defense is provided by a quantity of the well-known 40mm Bofors guns and, perhaps more significantly, by 80 Vulcan Air Defense Systems purchased from the USA. Half of these are self-propelled, carried on modified M113 armoured personnel carriers, while the other 40 are towed, mounted on wheeled carriages. The VADS consists of a multiple-barrelled 20mm Vulcan gun which has a maximum rate of fire of 3,000 rounds per minute. This is supported by a radar rangefinder, a night-vision sight, a conventional optical day sight, and a gyroscopic lead-computing unit which, on receipt of data on the course and speed of the aircraft, automatically offsets the sight to compensate for target motion. With a maximum range of about 5,500 yards, and an effective range of 3,000 yards, the VADS is a highly effective system.

Modern Gatling The six-barrelled 20mm Vulcan gun is Israel's main field air defense. It is a modern version of the famous Gatling machine gun. The six barrels each fire at only 500rpm, so avoiding overheating, but the gun as a whole produces a formidable 3,000 rounds per minute.

The lightweight missile in use is the American Redeye, of which 1,200 have been purchased. Redeye consists of three units — the launcher, the missile, and the launcher battery/coolant unit. The missile is sealed inside the launcher and is never removed except when fired. As well as holding the missile, the launcher carries the firing controls and the power and coolant channels necessary for target acquisition and firing. The launcher battery/coolant unit is inserted whenever action is imminent. There is a simple open sight.

The operator carries the equipment on his shoulder and, seeing a target, decides to engage it. He presses a trigger which actuates the battery/coolant unit, causing freon to flow to the seeker head of the missile and super-cool the infra-red detector. He points the sight at the target and infra-red radiation is picked up by the missile detector head. As soon as the missile is receiving sufficient infra-red signals to allow it to track, an audible signal is generated and a gyroscope in the missile is run up to speed and uncaged. On hearing the tone, the operator presses the firing trigger. The missile is ejected from the tube, coasts for a short distance so as to protect the operator from back-blast, and the main motor then ignites. The guidance system detects any difference between the missile's course and the source of infra-red energy, and steers the missile towards the source. Tracking and correction continues until the missile strikes the target and the warhead is detonated. If the missile misses its target, a self-destruction unit detonates the warhead, preventing it falling to the ground.

The Machine in Action

COMBAT EXPERIENCE LEADS all armies to develop their own individual 'style'; they have their own attitudes and their own ways of doing things, adopting modes of operation which, while still in total conformity with the accepted principles of war, nevertheless give the army and its operations a distinctive flavour of their own. Think of the German advance into Russia in 1941 — bronzed, lean and fit men in shirtsleeves striding along the dusty roads with a confidence born of successes, part of a grim and invincible fighting machine; of the British in the Western Desert in 1942, a happy-go-lucky crowd of individuals fighting what they thought to be the last of the 'gentlemen's wars'; of the Americans in Europe in 1944, chewing gum and smoking Lucky Strikes, with their characteristically informal discipline and fluid tactics; and of the Russians advancing on Germany in 1945, an implacable steamroller of men and machinery crushing all before it.

The image which comes to mind as far as the Israelis are concerned is somewhat different; dedicated men and women, mainly young, highly individual, with a vast degree of initiative and a confidence in their ability which sometimes seems to be carried to excess. But behind this is the conviction that they have succeeded before and they will succeed again, while, underlying that is the certain knowledge that, if they fail, then their nation itself will be totally destroyed. Another image is of resourcefulness, a willingness to take tactical and strategical risks, which many other armies would dismiss out of hand, a willingness to attempt manoeuvers and plans which have never been tried before but which promise rewards to the audacious man who first tries them.

All these characteristics can be seen in

The fortunes of war
Conflict has been part of the Middle Eastern legacy since the days of the Old Testament. Today is no different, though the weapons are more devastating than ever before. A white phosphorous shell explodes close to an Israeli M51 Sherman **(right)** — an incident during the Six Day War of 1967 — while the remains of an Egyptian infantryman **(below)** remind us that, in war, everyone is sometimes a loser.

Suez, 1956 Years after the event, it was revealed that Britain and France had prior knowledge of Israeli plans in 1956, all three powers having a common interest in humbling Nasser's Egypt. The map **(right)** shows the proposed Anglo-French assault plan, which began with air strikes by Canberra bombers, based on Cyprus **(far right)**, as the task force, headed by the aircraft carriers HMS Eagle and HMS Bulwark, approached Port Said **(below)**.

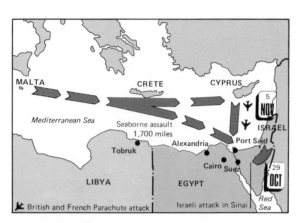

Short-lived success British paratroopers sitting on a captured Egyptian SU-100 assault gun after the invasion. International pressure soon forced Anglo-French withdrawal.

microcosm by studying the various battles which the Israelis have fought. Let us begin by taking a closer look at the 1956 campaign in the Sinai. In brief, the Israelis were threatened with a three-pronged attack from the unified forces of Egypt, Syria and Jordan, all three countries having avowed their intention of invading Israel. Opportunely, for the Israelis, the Egyptian nationalisation of the Suez Canal provoked Britain and France into an attack on the Canal Zone, an operation which took so long to mount that the Israelis were able to assess what was likely to happen, accurately calculate Egypt's responses, and proceed to make their own plans to capitalise on events as and when they took place.

At that time Israel's population numbered far less than it does today, so when the orders were given for secret mobilization on 26 October 1956, the call-up of some 100,000 reservists produced a total of about 150,000 men and women under arms. The procedure for mobilization was somewhat different to that used by the Israelis today and outlined earlier; key officers and NCOs were alerted by telephone or telegram, and they then passed the mobilization order on by word of mouth. Cumbersome though this sounds 12 brigades were fleshed out and ready for action within 12 hours.

The Israeli effort was to be concentrated in the Sinai, the key to which was the Mitla Pass through which runs the Aquaba-Suez road. The Sinai is a 27,000 square mile triangle of wasteland with few roads, so that control of the lines of communication was the territorial imperative. The decision was taken therefore to drop airborne troops to take and hold the pass, so preventing any delays there due to Egyptian action and opening up the Sinai to the Israeli column scheduled to advance from the area of Kuntilla right to the banks of the Suez Canal itself.

In accordance with this plan an armored brigade, led by General Sharon, crossed the border into Sinai shortly before nightfall on 29 October; an hour later a battalion of paratroopers was dropped about 15 miles east of the Mitla Pass. Operation Kadesh was under way. A second force now crossed the border behind Sharon's troops, turned north and drove north up the road to take Qusseima. This was a strategic road junction which gave the Israelis the choice of two routes by which the force could drive across the desert and reinforce the paratroopers at the Mitla Pass if required.

Sharon's force rapidly advanced on Thamad and disposed of the small Egyptian garrison there before dawn on 30 October. It then waited for an air drop of fresh supplies of fuel and ammunition and for a light airplane to evacuate the half-a-dozen wounded. While the Israelis waited, however, they were strafed twice by Egyptian

airplanes and then were radioed by the paratroopers with the news they were held up by artillery fire and had similarly suffered from air attack. While Sharon considered this, a reconnaisance aircraft reported that Egyptian columns were moving from Suez towards the Mitla Pass, and with this as the final argument Sharon moved forward at all speed.

In the meantime the Egyptians who had retreated from Thamad had dug in further along the road at Nakhl to reinforce the existing garrison. However, a sharp, concentrated artillery barrage from Sharon's 25-pounders forced them out of their positions and they decamped, abandoning a considerable stock of food and ammunition. By the evening Sharon had linked up with the paratroopers and on the following day, after a short, sharp engagement, the Mitla Pass was taken and defensive lines thrown up on the Suez side. Sharon's brigade now awaited the next phase of the operation.

Preparing for war Israeli Women's Corps trainees negotiate a smoke-obscured obstacle on a commando assault course in 1956.

117

Into battle The three-pronged Israeli invasion of the Sinai in 1956 **(below)** was highly successful, reaching its objectives at minimum cost. Israeli paratroopers played a vital part; two Dakotas **(right)** drop paratroops during the attack on the Mitla Pass, a key communications link.

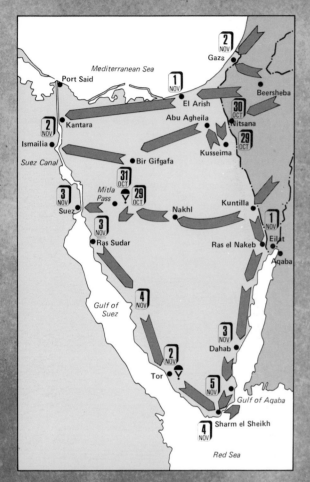

Meanwhile, the northern column — an armored brigade led by Colonel Ben-Avi and an infantry brigade under Colonel Harpaaz — had taken Qusseima and had swung east to attack Abu Agheila, the principal Egyptian position in the Sinai. This was a series of fortified ridges manned by two brigades — one armored. The Israeli plan was for the column to spread itself out, probe at the flanks, swing round and attempt to encircle the Egyptians. The Egyptians countered with their ex-Soviet T-34 tanks, which moved forward to stop the Israeli advance, the result being a tank battle which swayed back and forth for some 16 hours. While this was monopolising Egyptian attention, however, an Israeli reconnaissance company managed to slip around the southern flank and establish a blocking position on the Ismailiya road, preventing any reinforcements reaching the Egyptians. Then a detachment from Harpaz's brigade cut across the desert during the night and linked up with Sharon's brigade at Nakhl, so that by the morning of 31 October the entire southern half of the Sinai had been isolated from Egypt.

The second phase of the war now began with the advance of a motorized infantry brigade under Colonel Yoffe. This entered the Sinai near Eilat and headed down the coast road for Sharm el Sheikh, the lowest tip of the Sinai, on the Red Sea. Here, the Israelis varied their methods of resupplying their advancing troops, but the means

Overrun Israeli troops examine an Egyptian Archer self-propelled 17-pounder anti-tank gun, dug into a pit as part of the defences of Abu Agheila **(below)**.

they chose was equally ingenious. Landing craft had been brought overland from the Mediterranean coast on specially-built transporters. From the port of Eilat, these now ferried supplies and ammunition forward to rendezvous with the motorized column at pre-arranged points down the gulf.

In the north, the battle for Abu Agheila still raged, with the Egyptians putting up a valiant defence. An armored brigade and an infantry regiment were despatched from Ismailia to reinforce them but they were attacked and scattered by the Chel Ha'Avir before they reached Bir el Gifgafa. Though some of the force managed to reform and continue the advance, they were then halted by the Israeli blocking position, which had by now been reinforced by more of Ben-Avi's troops. The Egyptian response was to surprise even the Israelis by launching a counter-attack from Abu Agheila, pinning down the Israeli infantry with artillery fire while a force of T-34 tanks made its sortie. Though this move failed, it was a desperate night battle.

The next day — 1 November — another Israeli column, under Brigadier Laskov, then commander of the Armored Corps, bypassing the battle at Abu Agheila, struck north to take Raafah and then turned west to move along the coast road to threaten the tempting prize of El Arish, a major

Egyptian supply dump. This fell extremely rapidly since most of the Egyptian garrison had fled and the remainder surrendered with only a show of resistance. With El Arish safely under his control, Laskov pushed forward and by nightfall was in position just short of the Suez Canal.

During the day, too, a half-hearted Egyptian armored thrust against the Mitla Pass position was easily repulsed. As the Egyptians fell back, they were pursued by the Israeli first column troops, who, by the end of the day, had also nearly reached the canal, close to Port Tewfiq. They could have advanced to the canal itself, but an Anglo-French ultimatum halted them on a line 15km from its eastern bank.

The stalemate at Abu Agheila persisted, however, and was, by now, severely handicapping the flow of Israeli supplies to the front line. The result was that some Israeli units were being forced to use captured Egyptian T-34 tanks to replace their own casualties. In desperation the Israeli Chief of Staff, General Moshe Dayan, flew to the scene and took personal command. Under his direction, a fresh Israeli attack was launched. This succeeded in breaking through the first Egyptian defensive line, after which it was halted by a dogged Egyptian defense. This, however, was the Egyptians' last gasp, and during the night of 1/2 November they quietly melted away into the desert. The next morning the Israelis were able to resume their advance with little or no resistance and by nightfall the entire area was secured.

The final phase was the advance by a mechanized infantry brigade into the Gaza Strip to clear it of Egyptian troops and capture the city of Gaza. At the same time (2 November) an airborne battalion was dropped on the Egyptian airfield at Et Tur, on the Red Sea. Elements of Sharon's brigade moved down the west coats of the Sinai to link up with them and then continued to Sharm el Sheikh to meet the advance guard of Yoffe's brigade from Eilat.

In less than a week, therefore, one-third of the Egyptian Army had been soundly defeated in battle, most of the Egyptian Air Force had been shot down, and the entire Sinai was safely in Israeli hands. The cost for this was negligible — less than 200 killed and only four prisoners lost. But world opinion would not permit the victors to keep what they had gained; within a few weeks a UN peace-keeping force had begun replacing the Israelis.

This first campaign of the mature Israeli Army (in contrast to the motley force which had fought the 1948 war) shows the beginning of some of the tendencies which the world now sees as characteristic of Israeli operations. In the first place senior commanders were prepared to take risks which would rarely be considered in more

Racing to Suez Israeli troops **(below)** advance through a smokescreen, supported by Sherman tanks. A mechanized infantry column **(inset)** pauses close to a signpost to El Nakhl during the Sinai campaign.

Gaza falls Israeli Shermans, led by a Staghound armored car, advance into Gaza after its capture in November 1956 **(above)**. This was a key Egyptian position. Jubilant Israeli troops, carrying the Holy Scrolls of the Torah enter the town **(right)**, while the vanquished Egyptian commander, Major-General Fuad Dajawi, poses with his captors after the surrender **(far right)**.

established armies. There was a tendency to push forward at all costs, even with relatively small forces, hoping that sufficient gains would be made to allow adequate reinforcements to arrive and before any serious counter-attacks could be developed. Both characteristics can be seen in the side-stepping move around Abu Agheila and the establishment of a road-block by no more than a lightly armed reconnaissance company. A serious counter-stroke by the Egyptians would undoubtedly have wiped out this sortie, but, in the event, the Israelis got away with it. Some commentators pointed out that Sharon's brigade appeared to rest on its laurels far too long after taking Thamad, but they overlook the fact that the Israeli move had begun at 4.30pm the previous day and that the Israelis therefore had fought through the night. Rest was vital by the next morning, and the delay actually cost them nothing. But the overall impression is of 'speed with risks'. It is clear that the success or failure of the whole operation depended on the gamble of bringing it off within a week; the Israelis succeeded, but their transport echelons were on their last legs and the logistic supply system had been strained almost to breaking point. Had any more serious opposition been offered from the Egyptians — opposition which might have prolonged the conflict for another two or three days — it is hard to avoid the thought that the whole Israeli effort might have collapsed.

Spoils of war An Israeli technician checks the safety of captured Soviet anti-tank mines before storing them for future Israeli use **(top)**; the civilian **(right)** is holding an anti-tank shell for the ex-British 17-pounder Archer anti-tank gun.

Return to the Sinai The
map **(bottom)** shows the
Israeli thrusts into the Sinai
and Gaza Strip in June 1967.
Pre-emptive air strikes
smoothed the path of the
Israeli armor, which reached
the Suez Canal in four days.
Israeli mechanized infantry
in half-track carriers **(right)**
follow an armored
spearhead of Sherman
tanks into Sinai.

The Six-Day War of 1967 opened with the pre-emptive air strikes by the Chel Ha'Avir described in Chapter Four. But effective as these were, the fact remains that wars are not won by air power but by soldiers on the ground, defeating the enemy's forces and occupying the terrain, and the Israelis had to think of ground strategy as well as air power. The Egyptians had some 100,000 men and 1,000 tanks in Sinai by this time, having effectively driven the UN peace-keeping force out by political manoeuvering. Two armored divisions and five infantry divisions were distributed from the Gaza Strip across to Kuntilla, a distribution which made an excellent defensive line and which could also act as a jumping-off point for invasion of Israel by a number of routes. On the Jordan front there were seven infantry and two armored brigades — five of them deployed on the west bank of the Jordan — while further north, on the Syrian front, there was a 10-mile deep belt of wire and fortified positions occupied by 40,000 Syrian troops with over 250 tanks. Whichever way the Israelis looked there appeared to be a formidable force awaiting them, and it would need some astute strategy to survive this three-way threat.

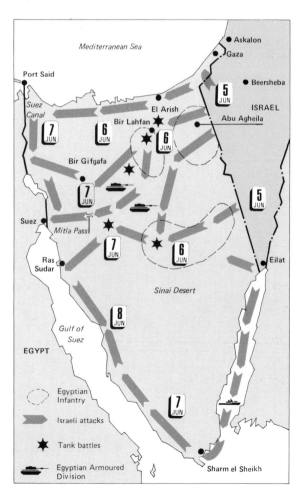

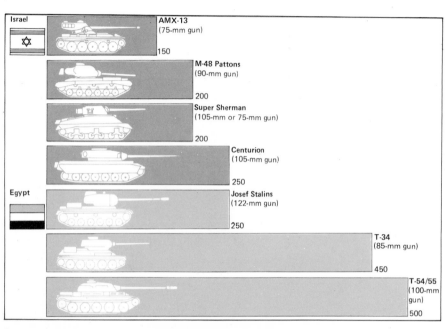

Israel		
	AMX-13 (75-mm gun)	150
	M-48 Pattons (90-mm gun)	200
	Super Sherman (105-mm or 75-mm gun)	200
	Centurion (105-mm gun)	250
Egypt	Josef Stalins (122-mm gun)	250
	T-34 (85-mm gun)	450
	T-54/55 (100-mm gun)	500

Balance of power The graph **(above)** shows the composition and relative strengths of Israeli and Egyptian armored forces prior to the Six Day War.

The build-up to war Israel's pre-emptive strike in 1967 completely nullified Arab advance planning, which had been considerable, if not entirely effective. UAR T55 tanks concentrate in the Sinai **(left)**, as Egypt's reserves are mobilized, Kuwaiti troops arrive to augment the Egyptian strength in the Sinai **(top left)** and troops of the PLO, armed with Soviet Goryunov machine guns, supplied by China, concentrate in the Gaza Strip, close to the Israeli border **(top right)**. Th Arab high command was confident of success; Field Marshal Amer **(below)** inspects his jet pilots at an advance airfield.

The tension mounts As the build-up to war continued, Israel's hero, Moshe Dayan **(right)** addresses his first press conference as Minister of Defense. He expressed confidence in Israeli victory and disclaimed the need for direct foreign military support. The super-powers, however, inevitably became involved. A Soviet destroyer **(below left)** on Mediterranean patrol observes Arab, Israeli and US Sixth Fleet movements, while **(right)** the USS Dyess, a Sixth Fleet destroyer, is assailed by demonstrators as she sails through Port Said harbor for the Suez Canal.

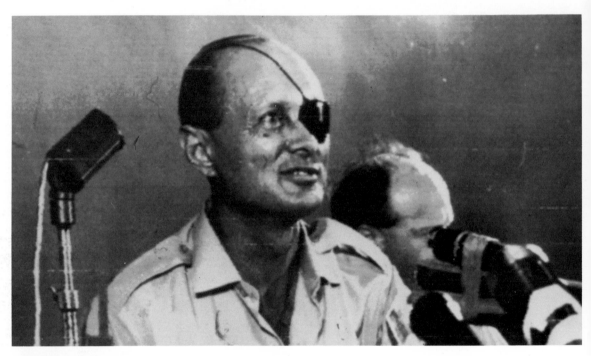

Outnumbered The chart **(right)** shows the huge material superiority of the Arab forces before the outbreak of the 1967 war. Egypt's tanks and aircraft alone outnumbered those of the Israelis.

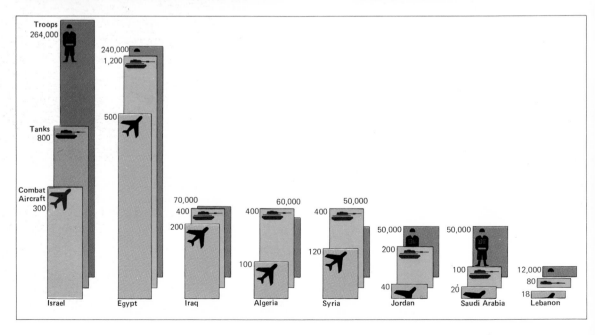

Israel — Troops 264,000; Tanks 800; Combat Aircraft 300

Egypt — 240,000; 1,200; 500

Iraq — 70,000; 400; 200

Algeria — 60,000; 400; 100

Syria — 50,000; 400; 120

Jordan — 50,000; 200; 40

Saudi Arabia — 50,000; 100; 20

Lebanon — 12,000; 80; 18

In effect Israel elected to duplicate Germany's Schlieffen Plan of 1914 insofar as this dealt with the problem of fighting on two fronts. The solution was to launch a massive attack on what appeared to be the most dangerous front while trusting to the enemy's inertia to delay the onset of attack on the other one, and deploying a small holding force to delay it for long enough to complete the first enemy's rout before turning to deal with the second. The Schlieffen plan failed because it was tactically adulterated, but it was a close-run thing; the Israelis made no such tactical mistakes.

The first Israeli move was to deal with the Egyptians, whom they knew to be the most dangerous of their foes. To do this, they began by a deception manoeuvre designed to lead the Egyptians to think that Israel would repeat its successful operations of 1956 — an attack across the Sinai coupled with an advance down the Gulf of Eilat. About a week before the war began Egyptian photo-reconnaissance aircraft detected an Israeli armour build-up in the area north of Kuntilla; in

Mobilization The Israeli response to the Egyptian build-up in the Gaza Strip was mobilization. Israeli Centurions in the Negev prepare for battle **(left)**, while Shermans churn up the dust on manoeuvers **(below)** in May 1967.

Backroom brains Israeli generals were prominent in the preparations for war. Generals Laskov, Yadin, Rabin, Makless, Tzur, Dayan and Dori inspect Israeli armor **(left, left to right)**. Rabin, the architect of Israeli victory, is seen in close-up **(right)**.

fact two of the three armored brigades were dummies.

The real Israeli main thrust was to be launched on the northern side of the Sinai. A brigade group under Brigadier Tal was to break into the Gaza Strip, storm Rafiah and then swing west to take El Arish. A second brigade group under Brigadier Yoffe would also strike towards the Gaza Strip, but in more westerly direction, so as to prevent reinforcements moving in Tal's direction; he would then join up with Tal to take El Arish. A third brigade group under Brigadier Sharon was to move to seize Abu Agheila and gain control of this vital junction.

The Gaza Strip was a formidable target. Its border was protected by an enormous minefield, behind which were the best part of two Egyptian divisions, well provided with anti-tank guns, dug-in tanks and artillery. But unless this formidable force was successful broken, the entire campaign could fail. As Tal said to his troops: "'If we are to win the war we must win the first battle . . . no matter what the casualties . . . we must succeed or die.'"

As the first Israeli air strikes smashed down on the Egyptian airfields, so Tal's troops rolled foward across the border of the Gaza Strip, led by two tank battalions. The minefield claimed several casualties, but the spearhead got through and headed for the town of Khan Yunis. The original plan was for the leading tank battalion of M48 Patton tanks to deal with the town while the second battalion, of Centurions, bypassed it to the south and headed for Rafiah. But as the attack neared Khan Yunis, it became obvious that the defences there were stronger than had been anticipated, and so both battalions attacked in a pincer movement which met in the town square. They handed the town over to the infantry to secure and then headed for Rafiah.

Rafiah turned out to be a hornet's nest; one-and-a-half brigades of infantry were liberally supported by about 150 Josef Stalin III heavy tanks and about 90 pieces of artillery. As the Israelis closed on the town, this formidable armament opened up to inflict massive damage. Since frontal attack was obviously suicidal, another lightning change of plan was maade. The Israelis

The war begins Israeli infantrymen check an Egyptian bunker in the Gaza Strip **(below)**; columns of Egyptian tanks **(above)** and transport **(above right)** burn after an attack by Israeli fighter-bombers.

Fresh supplies With its gun pointing rearwards, this Israeli Sherman rolls back from the battle area to stock up its ammunition during a lull in the fighting for the Gaza Strip in 1967.

Confidence and tragedy A Soviet built SU-100 assault gun of the Syrian Army moves forward to the Israeli border **(left)**. War claims casualties impartially, however, An Israeli pilot lies in front of the wreckage of his airplane in the Nile Delta **(center)**, the partially-furled parachute suggesting he was too low to successfully eject; the body of an Egyptian soldier lies alongside his Soviet B-11 recoilless anti-tank gun and box of ammunition in an ill-chosen position covering a road in the Gaza Strip **(near left)**.

swung their forces around Rafiah and returned to their planned line of advance at Sheikh Zuweid. There they surprised an Egyptian convoy en route to Rafiah and destroyed it. Charging on, Tal's armor now stormed the Jiradi Pass; this was held by the Egyptians, but the sheer speed of the Israeli advance caught them by complete surprise and most of Tal's force passed through without a shot being fired by the time the defenders woke up to what was happening. They managed to stop the last two Israeli Centurions, and, now thoroughly on the alert, greeted the following infantry with a hail of fire. The leading tanks, not realizing their supporting infantry was stuck, sailed on to the outskirts of El Arish, where they finally realized they were alone in enemy territory and halted.

Unfortunately the same sort of thing was happening further back along the line of advance. The Israelis had left a skeleton force to hold Khan Yunis, but, once the armor had departed, small parties of Egyptian and Palestinian snipers began to appear and slowly began to dominate the town. A body of paratroops, who had moved independently of the main force, had appeared at Rafiah from the south, where they had received such a hot welcome that they had been forced to call for a supporting air strike from the Chel Ha'Avir. The paratroopers also received further welcome aid from a column of Tal's tanks and the combined force eventually succeeded in breaking through the Egyptian defences. After this, the tired paratroopers turned north to clear the nuisance raiders out of Khan Yunis.

Gaza itself was fiercely defended and the Israeli armor had to shoot its way house by house into the center of the town. Gaza was formally surrendered on the morning of D + 2, but it was to be the next morning before all the holed-up snipers and nuisance raiders had been cleaned up and the Gaza Strip could be said to be firmly in Israeli hands.

To the south, Haron's advance to Abu Agheila was another 'at all costs' operation and it ran into trouble. Between his start line and his objective lay a strongly defended Egyptian position on the Um Katif plateau, which had been carefully laid out under the supervision of Soviet 'advisors'. A thick belt of mines and wire lay in front of three lines of trenches, which themselves were studded with concrete strongpoints; in direct support the Egyptians had positioned about 100 T-34 tanks and SU-100 self-propelled assault guns and missiles. Behind all this were six regiments of artillery manning Soviet 122mm howitzers.

Israeli intelligence claimed that the position was held by only a single Egyptian battalion; but two days before Sharon began his advance the garrison had been increased to a full division, and the initial headlong Israeli assault was broken up

Determination Israeli paratroops fire a captured .50 Browning machine gun from a former Egyptian bunker in the Sinai.

On the run An Israeli Super Sherman, with French turret and 75mm gun, dug into an ambush position alongside a wrecked train near El Arish **(below)**. An Egyptian MiG-17 fighter, shot down by Israeli airplanes near El Arish is simply wreckage, but, behind it, a Soviet BTR-152 armored personnel carrier has already been put to work by the Israeli victors **(below center)**. Barefoot prisoners do not run far in the desert — Egyptian troops, captured in the Gaza Strip, removing their boots before being taken to POW camps **(bottom)**.

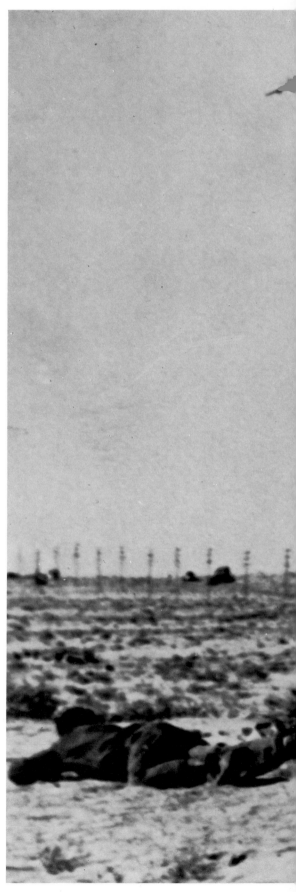

Roles reversed A rare occurrence after the air force's pre-emptive strikes — Israeli troops dive for cover as two Egyptian MiGs swoop on a motorized column in the Sinai advancing towards the Suez Canal.

Self-protection Reversing the gun, when withdrawing for re-supply, is a self-protective measure. Front-line infantry seeing tanks approaching with their guns forward shoot first and ask questions afterwards.

on the minefield and wire, with seven Centurion tanks put out of action. More air strikes were called in on the Egyptian position, while the surviving Centurions were pulled out and sent off to outflank the position and rejoin the line of advance. The second wave of tanks — M48 Pattons this time — then launched a second frontal assault, but this, too, was brought to a standstill by the mines and devastating anti-tank gunfire.

Sharon's next idea was to put in an infantry attack, coordinating it with a paratroop assault on the Egyptian artillery positions. The paratroops were to be landed by helicopter, but their selected landing zone was clearly visible to the Egyptians, who promptly severly mortared it. The result was that the assaulting party had to pull back to a safer landing area — which meant that they would have further to march to reach their objective. A call for further air strikes was turned down since the air force was fully committed elsewhere, and eventually Sharon decided on an old-fashioned preliminary artillery barrage and infantry assault at night.

By dawn the paratroopers were among the Egyptian artillery positions, but were pinned down by small arms fire, while the infantry assault had cleared a large area of the trench system. The road was clear and the paratroops were withdrawn. Though the infantry took the rest of the day securing the Um Kataif position, at least the armor was free to roll forward, turn south at the Abu Agheila junction and head for Quseima.

Once Sharon's troops had cleared the road, Yoffe's second armored brigade rolled forward to Abu Agheila and turned north to Bir el Lahfan. Here Yoffe's first brigade had arrived from the direction of Gaza and had run into strong Egyptian armored opposition. The second brigade now came up behind the Egyptians, and this sudden appearance in the rear was enough to break their resistance. The T-54s turned tail and headed for Egypt as fast as they could go.

The next objective was the Egyptian airfield at Djebel Libni. As soon as he had refuelled, Yoffe set off in that direction with one brigade, followed by Tal with his two. As they approached the airfield Yoffe turned left and Tal right to make a sweeping pincer movement which enclosed the whole of the airfield in an armored ring. This sweep was accompanied by an Israeli air strike on the field which dealt with several Egyptian tanks deployed around the perimenter. Those which were not hit by the air attack were driven from shelter and became targets for the Israeli tanks. The movement of their protecting armor unsettled the Egyptian infantry who, thinking their tanks were pulling out, decided to do likewise and set off for home. The Israelis settled down in their encircling positions for the night, resting

before a planned dawn attack, but by the time dawn arrived most of the defenders had evaporated and the airfield was taken with ease.

In this fashion, moving in well-defined bounds from one Egyptian position to another, the Israeli armor worked its way across the Sinai with two main objectives in view. These were to block the two main passes — the Ismailia and the Mitla — so trapping the Egyptians inside Sinai where they could be picked off in detail. Yoffe succeeded in reaching the Mitla Pass with a handful of Centurions and thereafter effectively closed it, assisted by the ever-attentive Chel Ha'Avir. Tal was less fortunate. The closure of the Mitla Pass meant that large concentrations of Egyptian armor now headed for the Ismailia Pass in such strength that Tal was unable to force his way close enough to seal off the Egyptian escape route. By this time Tal, too, was down to the last of his fuel and ammunition and his tanks were feeling the strain of continuous action. He withdrew from contact, rested his troops, called for fuel and ammunition, had some fresh tanks delivered, and in the morning of D + 4 was ready to begin again. Aided by air strikes with napalm, and with the superior armament of the Centurions telling against the T-54s, he made steady headway into the Egyptian positions. By 4.00pm over 40 Egyptian tanks had been destroyed for the loss of only two Israeli machines, and the Egyptians finally gave up the struggle and turned tail. By now, the Ismailia Pass was jammed by a crowded mass of armor and transport trying to get back to the safety of Egypt — a target which the Israeli aircraft could not miss. After high explosive and napalm had reduced the road to a continuous blazing ruin, Tal's armor was able to force its way through, shouldering aside the wreckage. On the morning of 9 June both Tae and Yoffe reached the Suez Canal, as did a motorized column on the coast road from El Arish. The southern front was secured.

The Israelis had hoped that the central front against Jordan would remain quiet, since it seemed likely that King Hussein would not inevitably follow Nasser's lead. On the evening of 5 June, however, Jordanian artillery began shelling Jerusalem and it was apparent that Hussein had decided to throw his hand in with the Egyptians and Syrians. The Israelis, therefore, began to put their plans for this sector into action. In essence, these called for an isolated sharp battle to regain control of the Old City of Jerusalem, whilst another battle would be fought to destroy the Arab Legion troops on the West Bank of the Jordan.

Suffice it to say that this is precisely what happened, though it was by no means a walk-over for the Israelis. Not only were the Arab Legion tough soldiers; they were also supported by Patton

The capture of Jerusalem
As the center of Biblical
Palestine, Jerusalem was a
major Israeli war aim, but
they met fierce resistance
from crack Jordanian
forces. The assault plan is
shown **(below right)**, a
Jordanian tank crew man

their anti-aircraft machine
gun **(below center)**, 105mm
self-propelled Jordanian
howitzers move into position
(bottom) and **(below left)**
the last ditch defence line —
Jordanian troops man a
recoilless anti-tank gun
overlooking the Notre Dame

de France church in
Jerusalem.

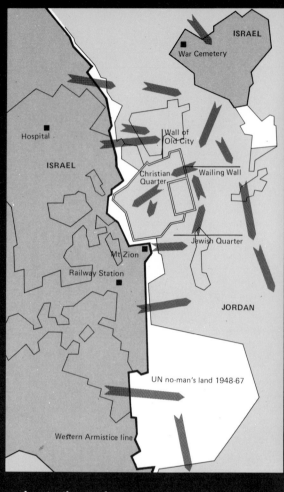

tanks similar to those operated by the Israelis. It
took a good deal of hard fighting before the twin
objectives were achieved, but fortunately the
Syrians, in the north, were disinclined to make
any move until (as they thought) the Israelis
would have been worn down by their battles on
the southern and central fronts.

The Syrians eventually thought that their time
had come and launched a series of severe artillery
bombardments. They had waited too long,
however. Once the southern and central fronts
were secure, the Israelis moved their formations
around and set about reducing the Syrian positions. A force of some 20,000 men and 250 tanks
was mustered and spread out to make four independent thrusts against the Syrians. One
brigade was to strike in the far north against
Banyas; slightly south of this an armored brigade
would take Zaoura and then turn and make for
Kuneitra, the Syrian sector headquarters. In the
central sector another armored brigade would attack towards Rawye, while infantry moved
around the eastern side of the Sea of Galilee, and a
paratroop brigade would attack the Golan
Heights near Tel Kazir.

The attacks went as planned, but the resistance
put up by the Syrians was surprisingly tough.

142

PRESS COLLECT UNIPIX LONDON PS4 = JERUSALEM OLD CITY JUNE 7
ISRAELI TROOPS IN CAPTURED JORDANIAN ARMY TRUCK DISPLAY

This year in Jerusalem!
Israeli troops tour Jerusalem in a captured Jordanian jeep, complete with 105mm recoilless gun and a picture of King Hussein on the radiator grill **(above)**. Other Biblical places similarly fell — **(far left)** Israeli troops in the center of Bethlehem and **(left)** an Israeli infantry column moving up towards the Mount of Olives.

Heavy artillery concentrations battered the armored thrust in the north and instead of the tanks simply cruising through the Syrian defences the battle degenerated into bloody hand-to-hand combat. By the end of the day (D+5) the Israeli forces had managed to break into the Syrian defences but they were running well behind schedule. Suddenly, at about noon the next day, Syrian resistance began to crumble all along the line; it was as if their morale reserves had been completely absorbed by the initial fighting. By 2.30pm the Israeli armor had entered Kuneitra to find it deserted. When air reconnaissance showed that the Golan Heights were undefended a force of paratroops was ferried forward by helicopter to occupy key points ahead of the infantry-armor advance.

Once again things had not gone the Arabs' way, and accordingly they called for a UN ceasefire. It came into effect at 6.30pm on D+6 and another war was over.

As with the 1956 war, the Israelis again showed that they were prepared to take enormous risks, reinforcing apparent failure and, against all the precepts, turning it into success. Although this tendency is still apparent today — a tendency which appalls Western generals and critics — there seems to be an element which is frequently overlooked. This is that the Israeli leaders, more than most generals in history, know their enemy. They have lived with and among Arabs, understand their mental processes, know their strengths and weaknesses and have a fine appreciation of their psychology. This allows them to take chances and liberties.

This familiarity, though, can easily breed contempt, as one instance in the 1967 war reveals. A column of Israeli tanks was ambushed by Jordamian armor and severely mauled, losing 17 tanks in the process. Having battled through, instead of waiting for air cover, the Israelis turned about and went through again, losing more thanks. Then, they called for air support!

On the other hand, Israeli appreciation of how Arabs react can sometimes crack a difficult problem. This was demonstrated in another incident on the Jordan front, when a group of Israeli Shermans were ambushed by Jordanian Pattons concealed in good defensive positions in olive groves. Two Israeli assaults got nowhere, but, instead of making a further attack, the Israelis fell back, leaving their burning tanks behind them. As they had foreseen, this apparent victory led the Jordanians to throw caution to the winds. Accordingly the Pattons roared out of their positions to pursue the supposedly beaten Israelis, who promptly turned round and, with a fluid battle to fight on terms of their own choosing, soon wiped out the entire Jordanian force.

Finally, we come to the Yom Kippur war of

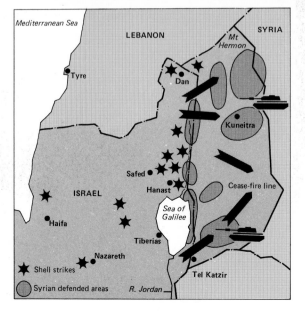

Against Syria The remarkable photograph **(above)**, taken through the periscope of a following tank, shows a Syrian T55 bursting into flames as the result of a strike by an Israeli shell. Israeli troops make a last-minute check of their tanks, after embarking them on transporters to be redeployed on the Syrian front **(right)**, while an Israeli patrol takes station in a Syrian olive grove. The radioman checks back for orders, while the anti-tank rocket squad keep an eye out for Syrian tanks **(far right)**. The map **(left)** shows the Israeli conquest of the Golan Heights.

Crossing the canal The Egyptian thrusts across the Suez Canal and the Israeli counter-moves are shown **(bottom)**. Israeli troops advance through the Sinai to take up defensive positions **(below right)**.

1973. In this case the war began with the roles reversed; it was the Egyptians who made the pre-emptive strike, with the Israelis being caught napping and consequently thrown on the defensive, at least initially. Indeed, Egyptian preparations were meticulous and impressive. They had planned the operation carefully, and against all the odds had managed to keep it secret. Equipment was moved into battle positions out of sight of Israeli border watchers, troops were trained and re-trained in attacks on facsimiles of the defensive Bar-Lev line the Israelis had established in Sinai, and wherever Israeli observers could observe Egyptian positions or troops, their every-day activity continued just as it had always done. Helmet-less soldiers wandered about, swam, played games and lazed in the sun, lulling the Israelis into a false sense of security, while behind them bridging equipment, armor, artillery, missiles and all the other elements of the planned offensive were stealthily moved into place. Above all, nobody in the Egyptian forces below the highest level knew when the attack was to begin; the Egyptians made their preparations, rehearsed and studied their operational orders, but not until the morning of 6 October did they know that the attack would take place that day.

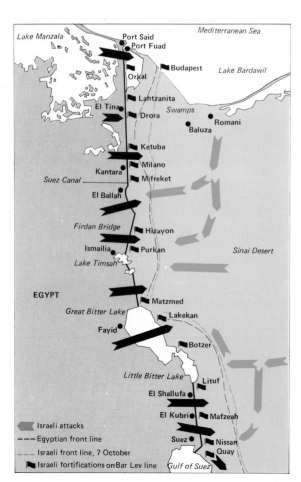

Lake Manzala · Port Said · Port Fuad · Mediterranean Sea
Budapest · Lake Bardawil
Orkal
Lahtzanita
El Tina · Drora · Swamps
Baluza · Romani
Ketuba
Kantara · Milano
Suez Canal · Mifreket
El Ballah
Firdan Bridge · Hizayon
Ismailia · Purkan · Sinai Desert
Lake Timsah
EGYPT
Matzmed
Great Bitter Lake · Lakekan
Fayid
Botzer
Little Bitter Lake · Lituf
El Shallufa
El Kubri · Mafzeah
Suez · Nissan Quay
Gulf of Suez

- Israeli attacks
- Egyptian front line
- Israeli front line, 7 October
- Israeli fortifications on Bar Lev line

On the Golan Heights the Syrian preparations
for a massive armored thrust were less well concealed, however. Israeli reconnaissance aircraft
were quick to detect the abnormal concentrations of armor and artillery. Although troop
movements and saber-rattling were (and still are)
a fact of life along Israel's borders, the information was enough to cause Moshe Dayan, now
Israeli Minister of Defense, to put the armed
forces on a general alert in late September and to
reinforce the northern front with an additional
armored brigade. Unfortunately, the Israelis
were for once let down by their intelligence. The
staff assessment of the reports from the various
fronts came to the conclusion that there was no
cause for alarm; the Arab movements they had
managed to detect were, in the Israeli opinion, entirely defensive. When the cabinet met a few days
before Yom Kippur the question of possible war
was not even raised. The Arabs had been soundly
beaten in 1967, they would not dare to start
another war, and even if they did they were so
militarily inept they would be bound to make a
hash of it.

On the evening of 4 October there was a sudden
exodus of Russian advisers and their families
from Egypt and Syria. Syrian armored and artillery formations suddenly began moving into
positions which made more sense as jumping-off
points than as defensive locations. When this information was received by the Israeli Chief of
Staff, General David Elazar, he was sufficiently
alarmed to order the armed forces to the 'highest
state of readiness'; leave was cancelled, men
already on leave recalled, and preparations made
for general mobilization.

The following evening, with the Jewish nation
about to enter one of its most solemn days of
religious observance, there was an emergency
cabinet meeting; Elazar argued for immediate
general mobilization, but the Prime Minister
(Mrs Golda Meir), the Deputy Prime Minister
(Yigal Allon), the Minister of Defence (Moshe
Dayan) and the Minister without Portfolio (Israel
Galili) were against this, their view being that a
provocative mobilization might even touch off
war. Moshe Dayan was sure that even if the Egyptians did attack they would need a whole day to
bridge the Suez Canal, and this would give the
Israelis enough time to mobilize, while if the
Syrian armor moved then Israeli air strength
could stop it in its tracks. On balance it would be
best to wait and see if Egypt attacked, for then, at
least, the Arabs would be branded as the aggressors.

In the morning, however, the Prime Minister
relented and approved the mobilization order. By
that time almost the entire nation was at prayer,
shops were closed, transportation had stopped
and the task of rounding up reservists was a for-

Egypt
680

Israel
488

Syria
410

2,000

2,600

1,700

650,000

300,000

000

Aircraft   Tanks   Troops

Yom Kippur Once the initial breaches were made, the Egyptians soon threw pontoon bridges across the canal and their mechanized columns began to move forward **(above)**. Golda Meir, the Israeli premier, announces the news of the attack **(bottom left)**. General Elazar, Israeli Chief of Staff, **(bottom center)** had argued for mobilization, but had been overruled, while Moshe Dayan **(bottom right)** crucially underestimated the Egyptian potential.

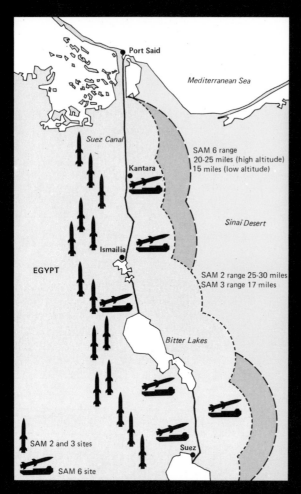

Within the map:

Port Said

Mediterranean Sea

Suez Canal

Kantara

SAM 6 range
20-25 miles (high altitude)
15 miles (low altitude)

Sinai Desert

Ismailia

EGYPT

SAM 2 range 25-30 miles
SAM 3 range 17 miles

Bitter Lakes

Suez

SAM 2 and 3 sites

SAM 6 site

midable one, with couriers combing synagogues and bus drivers having to be found to man buses and take reservists to their posts.

The Arab attack was launched at 2.00pm precisely that afternoon. Syrian tanks rolled across the Golan Heights in the North and Egyptian assault troops crossed the Suez Canal in small boats in the south. The crossing of the canal had been carefully planned; explosive charges planted by Egyptian frogmen blew down the sand walls on both sides in three places, whereupon the assault pioneers launched their boats and squads sped across the water to establish bridgeheads on the Israeli bank. More infantry followed them, as did Soviet PT-76 amphibious tanks which clambered from the water and headed straight for the first Israeli strongpoints. Flamethrowers and tanks soon made short work of these, and the first line of defences was rapidly breached. Now the Egyptian infantry fanned out and waited for the Israeli riposte, an attack by massed armor. Unfortunately for the Israelis the only armor they had in the area was a brigade of 200 Pattons. As these trundled forward to deal with the invaders they were greeted by a hail of wire-guided anti-tank missiles. Time after time the tanks tried to break through to re-take the

Bar-Lev strongpoints, and every time they were stopped, leaving more burning hulks behind them.

Seeing that these assaults were getting nowhere, the Israelis pulled their tanks and infantry back and set them to dig in in front of the key passes. If the lost ground could not be regained immediately, at least this move would block the Egyptian line of advance into Sinai. In their wake the Egyptian forward troops moved forward to a line about 10km from the canal. There, they too dug in with their anti-tank and anti-aircraft missiles and sat down to wait for the expected Israeli counterstroke. Their task now was to hold off the Israelis while bridges were thrown across the canal to allow the mass of Egyptian armor and artillery to move forward.

The canal crossings took place far faster than Moshe Dayan had foreseen, due to the Egyptian use of high-pressure water cannon to wash down the sand ramparts and then the rapid deployment of Soviet PNP bridging equipment, which could be laid at the astonishing rate of 15 feet per minute. By nightfall, 10 bridges had been flung across the canal and during the hours of darkness five Egyptian divisions and 500 tanks crossed into Sinai.

On the morning of 7 October the Chel Ha'Avir went into action, their Phantoms and Skyhawks roaring in to destroy the Egyptian bridges. Here, the Egyptians had another surprise in store. They had packed the canal area with Soviet SA-6 anti-aircraft missile batteries, whose missiles were totally new to the Israelis. As a consequence their airplanes were not equipped to deal with the problem, though, even if they had been, the normal deception devices would have been useless against the SA-7 shoulder-fired missiles carried by the Egyptian troops in the field. These were fitted with infra-red heat-seeking warheads, against which electronic countermeasures were useless. The end result was that 60 per cent of the attacking airplanes were shot down.

In hindsight, it is plain to see that, had the Egyptians forced their way forward and stormed the passes, they would probably have broken the Israeli army. Here, the influence of their Soviet instructors showed. The Egyptians had assimilated some basic Soviet tactical doctrines, one of which is that consolidation comes before advance. So, instead of thrusting ahead, they busied themselves with digging in their defensive line and preparing to receive an Israeli counter-attack. Furthermore they were reluctant to move out from underneath the protection of the missile batteries around the canal area and expose themselves to the might of the Israeli Air Force.

In the north the Israelis had been more on the alert, so, when 30,000 Syrians, backed by nearly 1,000 tanks, came rolling forward, they were not

October 1973 The Yom Kippur campaign went badly for the Israelis at first. Two Egyptian officers examine a captured Israeli M48 tank **(below)**; another M48 and the regimental commander's signal vehicles watch an engagement **(left)**. Perceptive leadership pulled Israel through — Brigadier Avraham 'Bren' Adan **(left)** and General Aluf Israel Tal both featured prominently in the 1973 campaigns **(far left)**.

Battle scenes Israeli mechanized infantry move past a burning line of Egyptian transport **(above)**. The yellow panel distinguishes the APC for friendly airplanes. Syrian troops posed on top of the wreckage from Israeli Skyhawk and Phantom jet fighters, shot down near Damascus **(right)**. The remains of the 20mm Vulcan gun carried by the Skyhawk can be seen near the camera. An Israeli 175mm long-range gun fires during the 1973 campaign **(top right)**.

taken by surprise. Covered by an intense artillery barrage, Syrian mine-clearing tanks led the way through the Israeli minefields, while bridging tanks established crossings over the anti-tank ditch which marked the border. Once across, the Syrians spread out and advanced in a massive line, backed up by infantry in armored personnel carriers. Israel's opposing Centurions and Pattons began cutting the attack to ribbons with their superior 105mm guns. The Israeli Air Force joined in, but, as in Sinai, they ran into intense missile fire, losing 34 aircraft in the first afternoon of fighting. Eventually they managed to detect and knock out the missiles' radar and fire control installations, but over 80 airplanes were lost before air superiority was achieved. Nevertheless, the Syrian columns were devastated by bombs and napalm, and by superhuman efforts the defenders on the Golan Heights managed to hold off the Syrian attack until the first Israeli reserves could get into position and take some of the strain.

Sunday 7 October was the critical day on the Golan front. The Syrians had brought up another 300 tanks from their reserves, and as dawn broke they resumed their push. In spite of every Israeli effort, with tanks burning all around, the sheer weight of numbers began to tell. But just as the

On the Syrian front The map **(below)** shows the action on the Syrian front in 1973. The initial Syrian attacks across the Golan Heights were eventually held. The Minister of Defense in the heart of the action — Moshe Dayan in a front line observation post on the Golan Heights **(bottom)**; Israeli Centurions prepare to move off after stocking up with ammunition **(right)**. The discarded packing lies in the foreground.

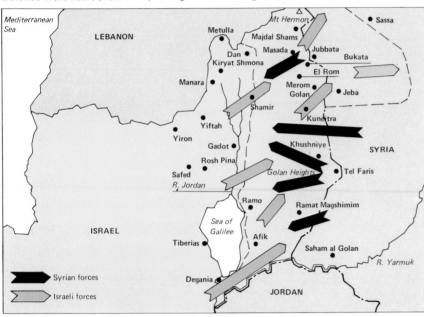

Mediterranean Sea

LEBANON

Mt Hermon · Sassa

Metulla · Majdal Shams

Masada · Jubbata

Dan · Bukata

Kiryat Shmona

El Rom

Manara · Merom Golan · Jeba

Shamir

Yiftah · Kuneitra

Yiron · Khushniye · SYRIA

Gadot

Rosh Pina

Safed · Golan Heights · Tel Faris

R. Jordan

Ramo · Ramat Magshimim

Sea of Galilee

ISRAEL · Afik

Tiberias · Saham al Golan

R. Yarmuk

Degania · JORDAN

▶ Syrian forces
▷ Israeli forces

Syrians appeared to have broken through the defensive line, so the first reserve Israeli tank formations began to appear on the heights, having driven through the night. The Syrians were held through the day, and by Monday morning the Israelis had built up their strength so that they were ready to go over to the offensive.

In the Sinai, the Israeli counter-offensive had begun at the same time, with some 700 tanks advancing against the Egyptian positions, accompanied by artillery fire from both sides. To everyone's surprise the Israelis were routed and the front settled down into a stalemate as each side waited for the other to attack.

The Russians, thinking perhaps that one more push might do the trick, now began ferrying more weapons to Egypt. Artillery, ammunition and missiles began arriving by air, while shiploads of tanks and fighter aircraft started to dock at Alexandria. By the end of the week some 4,000 tons of supplies reached the Egyptian supply dumps from Soviet sources. Golda Meir appealed

Counting the cost The material cost of war is enormous, as these four pictures demonstrate. An Egyptian truck blazes after being straafed by Israeli jets **(above)**, a burned-out Syrian jeep on the Golan Heights **(right)**, Syrian equipment wrecked by Israeli artillery fire **(far right)** and a crippled Syrian tank, its turret blown off by Israeli artillery, **(right center)** all prove the point. Israeli gunners are extremely accurate.

Accidents will happen This Syrian tank on the Golan Heights **(above)** appears to have missed its footing while trying to cross an emergency bridge.

to the USA to redress the balance which, after a brief delay, the Americans agreed to do. New fighter aircraft appeared, together with other much-needed weapons, such as TOW anti-tank missiles, anti-radar and air-to-air missiles, electronic countermeasures equipment and guided bombs.

On the Sinai front, the commanding Israeli officers disagreed as to how the battle should proceed, and it was not until Moshe Dayan recalled General Bar-Lev from retirement and put him in command that the bickering died down. Another retired officer recalled to the colors was General Sharon, who, in his service days, had made a particular study of the problems involved in crossing the Suez Canal from east to west. He had even gone so far as to prepare hard-standings for vehicles, parking areas, and had the Canal's sand walls weakened and secretly marked. After much argument, he was permitted to try out his plan, with three mechanized brigades (their tank strength depleted to about 200), a mechanized parachute brigade, and a force of assault pioneers.

On Sunday 14 October, the ninth day of the war, Sharon's force assembled to hear his orders. His plan was to create a diversion by using one armored brigade to make a feint against the Egyptians, while another seized a critical road which would permit the third brigade and the rest of the force to reach the canal. Tanks and paratroopers would be ferried across the canal to establish a bridgehead, after which a bridge would be laid, the rest of the force would cross, and then the whole force would rampage up the west bank of the canal, wiping out missile battieres and anything else they found.

The diversionary force drew the Egyptian fire so well that the diversion turned into a full-scale tank battle which raged for two days. It ended with the Israeli brigade being almost wiped out, but it had performed its allotted task. The result was that the rest of the force was able to get to the canal, though well behind schedule. The initial pioneer crossing was made at 1.00am on Tuesday 16 October and met no opposition, all eyes being on the furious fight raging around the diversionary brigade. Because of a subsequent delay, however, it was not until 6.00am that the first Israeli supporting tanks began the crossing. By this time the Egyptians had been alerted and the first ferries were sunk by their artillery. Egyptian tanks appeared but were immediately knocked out by the Israeli troops holding the bridgehead. After this, there was no more Egyptian interference and 30 tanks and 2,000 troops were successfully established on the west bank, of the canal by 9.00am.

One aspect of Sharon's planning now paid off. He had directed his attack at the junction of two Egyptian formations. This is traditionally a weak

Counter-attack at Suez
This map shows the Israeli counter-attack against the Egyptian bridgeheads on the far bank of the Suez Canal. The Egyptian positions on the east bank were eventualy encircled.

Israeli riposte Israeli tanks are ferred across the Suez Canal on a Unifloat raft **(above left)**, following plans laid by Yigal Allon, deputy premier, General Bar-Lev, architect of the Bar-Lev line and Chief of Staff, and Major-General Yeshaya Gavish, commander of the southern Sinai district, seen **(left to right)** studying the west bank of the Suez Canal **(left)**.

The Israelis cross An Israeli tank parks opposite a mosque after crossing the Suez Canal **(above)**, while a group of Egyptian soldiers sits in the sun after capture **(right)**. Resting in the shade of the trees, the crew of an Israeli Centurion pose for a photographer after successfully completing their crossing **(above right)**.

spot in any battle array, but more so in this particular situation since the Egyptians suffered from poor communications and inadequate liaison between units. For over a day Sharon was left alone to reinforce his position, and he augmented that by sending out raiding parties to do whatever damage they could to any Egyptian installations they could find. Within hours they had found and destroyed four missile command centers. This hole in the protective umbrella meant that the Israeli Air Force was finally able to break through the Egyptian defenses to establish complete air superiority.

By Wednesday, the canal had been bridged and three fresh tank brigades, led by General 'Bren' Adan, were able to cross to be in place to repulse an Egyptian attempt to destroy the bridgehead that night. With 8,000 men and 200 tanks, the Israelis 'in Africa' now spread north and south from their crossing point and began systematically destroying every Egyptian gun battery and missile site they could find. The Egyptians now realised the acute peril of their position; with this force rampaging along the west bank of the canal, their bridges were at risk and their supply lines were about to be cut.

On the Golan Heights the Israelis were now thrusting the Syrians back; Iraqui troops had been thrown in, but they were of poor quality and ill-prepared and their appearance merely added to the Arab casualty lists. On 13 October, after much indecision, King Hussein sent an armored brigade to join in the battle. It arrived on 16 October, just as the Syrians had managed to establish and hold a defensive line, and immediately joined in a combined Syrian-Iraqui-Jordanian counter-attack. The Jordanian Centurions, handled with great skill and verve, advanced in a concentrated spearhead, and, for the loss of only 14 out of the 150 tanks, punched a hole clean through the Israeli line. Then, as success seemed in sight, the whole thing fell apart through sheer in-competence. The Iraqui artillery, which should have fired an opening barrage, opened fire half an hour late, by which time the Jordanian armor was right in the target area. Syrian fighter-bombers, brought in to soften up the Israelis in front of the Jordanian tanks, mistook their targets and strafed the Iraqui infantry which were moving up in support. The whole operation became so chaotic that it was abandoned, the Jor-danian armor pulled back, and the Israelis were able to regain their positions and then go over to the offensive once more.

It was at this point that it began to dawn on the Arab commanders that they were once again fac-ing the possibilities of defeat. At the same time both the USSR and USA began to realise that if the increased level of their support was bringing the grave danger of a major confrontation between the two super-powers, since eventually one or other of their 'client' states was bound to lose. The final impetus towards peace, as far as the West was concerned, was the announcement by Saudi Arabia that oil supplies would be withheld from the West until peace was restored in the Middle East. A cease-fire was hurriedly arranged, as the Soviets, for their part, moved to cut off their flow of weapons to Egypt and Syria. Unfortunately the news of the cease-fire was slow to percolate down to the troops in the field, particularly the Egyp-tians in Sinai who had no idea of what the real situation was and could see no need for a cease-fire at all. The original cease-fire was supposed to take effect on 22 October, but Egyptian and Israeli forces continued to fight around the canal until 25 October. Even then there were still some 20,000 Egyptians trapped in the Sinai, and Israel showed no inclination to let them evacuate their positions until they formally surrendered.

The 1973 war was a salutary lesson for the Israelis. Their short and successful campaigns in 1956 and 1967 had given them, to put it bluntly, swollen heads; they were convinced that they on-

ly had to appear on the horizon and the Egyptian and Syrian troops would turn and run; that the Arabs were incapable of fighting; and that their commanders were incapable of planning. The 1973 war disabused them of these ideas, and since that time there is little doubt that they have had a good deal more respect for the Arab armies and have not allowed themselves to slip into the sort of complacency which allowed them to be taken by surprise in 1973.

On the other hand, it also showed that, although the Israeli forte is mobile warfare, the Israelis are still capable of fighting less glamorous but more demanding, types of battle. Their delay-ing actions in Sinai and on the Golan Heights were extremely bitterly fought defensive actions, in which they performed admirably. There is little doubt that had the super-powers not intervened, the rout of the Egyptian and Syrian forces would have been complete and devastating.

As a result something like a negotiated peace was eventually achieved between Israel and Egypt, though the agreement between the two powers was bitterly condemned by other Arabs.

The Machine Today

ALMOST A DECADE HAS PASSED since the cease-fire of the Yom Kippur war brought an end to open conflict between Israel and its Arab neighbors in 1973, but this can hardly be called an era of peace. Sporadic outbursts of terrorism, border clashes, shelling and rocket attacks across the borders into Israeli settlements and the inevitable Israeli reprisals — all have continued in an irregular pattern as dissident Arab elements have probed at the defences of Israel, sometimes with official backing, sometimes without. In addition, the Yom Kippur war brought Israel a vast increase in the number of Arabs under its rule, in the so-called 'occupied' territories, who were also a possible source of unrest. As a result the Israeli Defence Force has never lapsed into a 'peacetime' attitude of mind but has constantly been on the alert for action. From time to time it has been forced to take more positive steps and attack terrorist bases in Arab territory, raids mounted either by air forces or by ground troops.

Israel's principal opponent in this hit-and-run type of warfare has been the Palestine Liberation Organization, operating from Lebanon. Most casual newspaper readers think the PLO is merely a collection of terrorists and guerillas, but it is, in fact, an army of considerable size, well equipped with modern small arms and heavy weapons by its sympathisers in Libya, Saudi Arabia, Syria, Hungary and the USSR. An Israeli intelligence estimate early in 1982 determined that the PLO were in possession of 80 tanks, 300 pieces of artillery and multiple rocket launchers, SAM-7 shoulder-launched anti-aircraft missiles, ZSU-23-4 self-propelled anti-aircraft guns, two light patrol boats and a number of helicopters. Some 5,000 PLO troops manned this equipment in South Lebanon, a build-up which had been going on since 1970.

Into Lebanon The Israeli 'Peace in Galilee' operation was designed to crush the PLO swiftly, but it soon turned into a drawn-out involvement that aroused opposition in Israel itself. An Israeli armored personnel carrier advances into Lebanon at the start of the operation **(below)** and Israeli troops push towards Beaufort Castle, a PLO stronghold **(bottom)**.

Constant battle The PLO have kept Israeli forces in a constant state of readiness. An armored personnel carrier moves off at night to carry out a raid against PLO bases in Lebanon.

Civilian alert Israeli settlers on the west bank of the Jordan faced constant attack. Here, Ester Baruch, nine months pregnant, waits outside the kindergarten in Kiryat Arba, loaded submachine gun in hand.

South Lebanon, in fact, was turned into virtually a Palestinian state, the PLO usurping the powers of the civil government and making free with food, water, medical supplies and every other aspect of life. PLO guns and rockets were positioned to fire into northern Israel, camps for the training of more PLO troops (and also for the training of international terrorists) were set up, and fortifications built against a possible Israeli attack.

Israel came face to face with the demands of international terrorism on several occasions in the 1970s and 1980s. Probably the most significant incident took place in July 1976, when the world was given a remarkable demonstration of Israeli determination and military efficiency in an operation of a totally different kind to the ones normally associated with the Israeli armed forces. At the end of June, pro-Palestinian terrorists hi-jacked a French airliner and forced it to fly to Entebbe in Uganda. There, without interference from the Idi Amin regime, over 100 passengers — a number of them Israelis — were held hostage, while their captors demanded that the Israeli government make concessions to the Palestinians in exchange for the hostages' lives.

The Israeli government firstly announced it would not yield to force. Realizing, however, that time would be needed to see if a rescue could be attempted, the Israelis pretended to negotiate, while a major operation to free the hostages was put in train.

As a start, a number of RF-4E Phantom photo-reconnaissance aircraft overflew Entebbe and pin-pointed its defences, the locations of various aircraft and the position of the hostages and their captors. Then, just before the final deadline, four Hercules C-130 transports, one converted into a flying fuel tanker, protected by a flight of F-4E Phantom fighters, set out for Entebbe by a roundabout route covering almost 2,500 miles.

On arrival at Entebbe, three of the transports cut their engines and landed silently, taxi-ing to a quite corner of the airfield. The rear ramps opened and, from the first Hercules, rolled a peculiar convoy. It consisted of a black Mercedes limousine, bearing the licence plates of President Idi Amin, followed by two buff-coloured Land Rovers carrying men dressed as Palestinians and armed with AK47 rifles. The assembly duplicated the usual entourage of President Amin, who used Palestinian Arabs as his personal bodyguard.

The three-vehicle convoy approached the terminal to be saluted by the Ugandan troops there. Amin had frequently visited the hostages, the deception was helped by night and there was no reason for the Ugandans to suspect that all was not what it seemed. But, while the diversion was taking place, Israeli troops were disembarking from the C-130s. Some began preparing explosive

The face of defiance A PLO guerrilla takes aim with his Soviet RPG-7 anti-tank rocket launcher just outside Beirut **(right)**.

The extremes PLO weaponry differs widely. An extemporized anti-aircraft gun **(above left)**, built by mounting a four-barrelled 14.5mm heavy machine gun on the back of a truck, prepares to take on Israeli jets. The Soviet twin 37mm anti-aircraft gun **(above right)** is in action in Beirut

Villain and heroes Idi Amin, President of Uganda, provided support for the PLO while posing as an honest broker between the Israelis and the Entebbe terrorists **(below left)**. Israeli crack paratroop commandos were the heroes of Entebbe **(below right)**.

The Entebbe raid The stalwart Hercules **(above)** made the raid **(below left)** possible. The map **(right)** shows the routes to Entebbe.

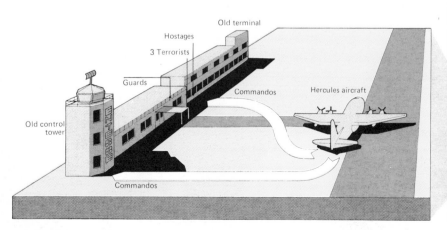

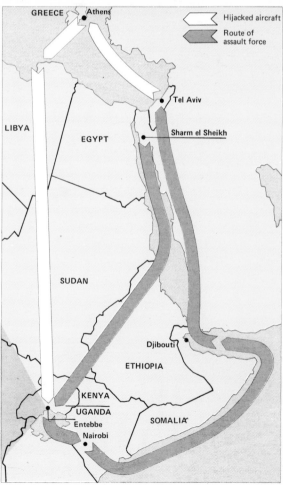

The necessities of war
Troops of the UN peace-keeping force in Lebanon **(far left)** stand aside impotently as the Israeli advance into Lebanon passes their outpost. Israeli jet fighters strike at PLO positions near Tyre **(above)** and at West Beirut **(left)** as the advance continues.

Front line An Israeli 175mm gun bombards Beirut **(below)**. The gunners in the foreground are manhandling 67kg shells, while the cartridge bags can be seen between the two men on the right. An Israeli infantry section on the advance **(bottom)**: most of the section are taking care to keep behind the crest, but the radio operator appears to be risking his neck.

charges to draw the Ugandans away from the airport building, while others made ready to destroy the Ugandan Air Force MiG fighters on the airfield.

Suddenly the whole airfield erupted. Explosive charges detonated, Ugandan troops ran from the terminal and started to investigate, the MiGs suddenly exploded and the 'Palestinians' in the Land Rovers leapt out and, with their fellow Israeli commandos, who had crept up in the darkness, stormed the airport buildings. Shouting to the hostages to throw themselves flat, the Israelis opened fire, shooting down the terrorists. Ugandan troops in the control tower attempted to intervene and one of their shots killed the Israeli commander. However, they were soon silenced by accurate Israeli return fire.

The hostages were rapidly bundled into the C-130s and flown to Nairobi in Kenya, where an Israeli Boing 707, outfitted as a hospital plane, was waiting. One C-130 remained at Entebbe and collected the last of the raiding party. It then took off to join the others at Nairobi. The total time that had elapsed from start to finish of the raid was no more than 53 minutes.

Parallel to this, PLO activity against the Israeli homeland continued to escalate. In March 1978 the 'Coastal Road Massacre' took place, in which a PLO guerilla force killed 33 Israeli civilians and

wounded a further 82. In retaliation, Operation 'Litani' was mounted by the IDF. In this operation a number of mobile IDF columns scoured South Lebanon from the northern Israel border to the Litani river, destroying PLO bases and chasing the PLO troops northwards. This operation lasted seven days, and, after it, a United Nations Peace-Keeping force (UNIFIL) moved into the area under the mandate of Security Resolution 425, set-

The air raids, however, seem to have been the goad needed to push the PLO into full-scale overt aggression. No sooner had the Israeli aircraft returned to their bases than PLO artillery and rocket launchers launched intensive bombardments of Israeli settlements along the border. On the following morning the attacks continued, and Israeli artillery began firing back at the PLO batteries. This was followed by Israeli Air Force strikes on PLO positions, which in turn led to increased PLO bombardment of civil areas. Now the Israelis began systematic air attacks on every known PLO location north of the border, seeking out ammunition dumps, supply lines and artillery positions in the face of heavy Palestinian anti-aircraft fire.

Even so, the PLO bombardment grew in intensity with hundreds of shells arriving every hour, and the Israeli northern settlements were rapidly becoming completely untenable. On Sunday

Israel's allies Lebanese Christian militia take up their positions around the ruins of Beaufort Castle, having been given control of the position by the Israeli Army **(bottom)**. Israeli Prime Minister Menachim Begin hands over the castle to Major Haddad, watched by Defense Minister Sharon **(inset)**.

The battle for Beirut A captured Syrian T-62 tank **(top left)** has been backed into a bulldozed pit and partly covered with earth to make a fixed artillery piece to shell PLO positions. An 81mm mortar fires from the open hatch of an armored car **(below left)**, Israeli troop carriers move out of the Lebanon Parliament Building ground **(top right)** and infantry dismount from their carrier as they approach Beirut airport **(below right)**.

morning, therefore, the Knesset ordered the army to carry out its long-planned Operation 'Peace in Lebanon'.

The Israelis had planned the attack long in advance, just as the PLO had also planned its defence. Indeed, given the assumption that at some time or other such an operation would have to be launched, the tactical plan was obvious, since there was little or no room for cleverness. However, there is a difference between theoretical tactics and those actually put into execution, so, though the PLO predicted the Israeli moves fairly accurately, it was totally unprepared for the speed with which the IDF took action and the firepower it had at its disposal.

The Israeli government's original directive to the IDF Staff had three principal clauses. The first aim was to clear the PLO out of the Lebanon border are, so that none of the civil population in Galilee was within range of PLO weapons; the second directive was to avoid any unnecessary entanglement with Syrian regular forces, who controlled a large area of northern Lebanon; and the third was to avoid involving the Lebanese civilian population. In broad outline, the IDF plan was to divide its forces into three fast-moving columns, each with their own air and artillery support, which would strike up the main routes into Southern Lebanon and aim for the main PLO centers. One column moved up the coast road,

aiming at Tyre, one moved from the extreme north of the Hula Valley northwest to take Nabatiye, and another moved northwest from roughly the same area in the direction of Hesbia. The center column was to divide, part of it crossing towards the sea to meet the first column as it neared Sidon, the remainder striking north towards the Beka'a Valley. The third column would simply continue northwards, acting as a backstop to trap any terrorists fleeing from the other two columns.

At 11.ooam that Sunday morning, the Israeli columns moved across the border, brushing aside the toothless forces of UNIFIL. On the coast road, the spearhead was composed of Centurion

tanks followed by mechanized infantry in M113 APCs, all backed by close support from Kfir and Skyhawk fighter-bombers. Soon a fierce battle was raging around Tyre and the nearby Rashidiye Camp, a PLO stronghold. The Israeli column pinned down the defenders and, leaving a holding force, moved to a flank and bypassed Tyre, heading north for their next objective. In the central sector another Centurion-led force headed for the vital Akiya bridge over the Litani river, secured it, and moved against Nabatiye, which held the principal command and operational center of the PLO.

The right-hand column had the difficult task of attacking the PLO stronghold in Beaufort Castle.

The battle continues
Palestinian guerrillas keep up the struggle with a four-barrelled ZPU heavy machine gun, mounted on a truck as a mobile air defence unit **(top left)**. Smoke billows from the PLO ammunition dump in the Beirut sports complex, after an Israeli naval bombardment **(below left)**, a troop of Israeli Merkava tanks pause for respite outside the Lebanese National Museum **(top right)** and an Israeli artilleryman loads a BM24 rocket launcher, accompanied by a souvenir 'liberated' from a wrecked Beirut boutique **(bottom right)**.

The fight for the airport A confident PLO fighter, armed with an RPG-7 anti-tank rocket launcher, about to take up a position at Beirut airport **(below left)**. An Israeli M113 armored personnel carrier, seen across the remains of a burned-out Middle Eastern Airlines Boeing 707, rolls in to crush opposition **(bottom left)**, while Israeli troops salute as their flag is lowered over the airport **(below center)**, as they leave to allow US marines of the peace-keeping force to take over. The main runway can be seen in the background in this photograph of the remains of a Syrian T62 tank **(below right)**, wrecked in the battle.

Last stand Mobile warfare, Palestinian style. A group of PLO guerrillas, with RPG-7 rocket launcher and RPK machine gun, tour the streets of Beirut in a commandeered vehicle.

Beaufort stands at the edge of a high plateau and commands a wide area of the plain below it. Built in the 12th century by the Crusaders, it has a long and bloody history, but for all its antiquity it is still a difficult nut to crack, with precipitous slopes guarding most of the approaches. IAF fighter-bombers kept up a continuous series of attacks, while self-propelled artillery was driven into a postion to begin a bombardment. Helicopters lifted infantry into long-stop positions behind Beaufort, from which they moved out to take several PLO blocking force positions. Finally, during the hours of darkness, hand-picked Israeli infantry silently scaled the cliffs in front of the castle and moved to the attack. After fierce hand-to-hand fighting, the PLO garrison was routed and the castle secured. This removed a constant threat to the valley below and allowed Israeli supply columns to move up safely in support of the armored columns.

The same night, Israeli armor and mechanized infantry made an amphibious landing at the mouth of the Awali river, north of Sidon. Supported by missile-carrying attack boats, the landing craft reached the shore without damage and unloaded their troops, which then swung south to take Sidon in the rear as the coastal column arrived on the other side.

While the coastal column kept advancing, the inland forces were moving cautiously, bearing in mind their directive to avoid confrontation with the regular Syrian forces. The Syrians, however, were feeling their strength. They had moved vast concentrations of armor, artillery and anti-aircraft missiles into the Beka'a Valley and they were now providing a refuge for PLO forces fleeing from the Israeli advance. PLO artillery inside the Syrian enclaves was actually bombarding the Israeli forces and also shelling northeastern Galilee. In spite of Israeli requests to move the PLO out, the Syrians decided to make an issue of it, and the Israeli command therefore changed its plans. While the coastal column continued northwards to ring Beirut and pin several thousand PLO terrorists inside the city, the remainder of the army swung eastwards and prepared to give battle to the Syrians.

The central Israeli column now confronted the Syrian 1st Armored Division in the Beka'a Valley. Meanwhile, the eastern column had struggled northwards along mountain tracks to reach a position overlooking the Beirut-Damascus road, so cutting the Syrians off from their rear.

At noon on Wednesday 9 June, the Israeli Air Force appeared in strength over the Beka'a Valley and, in a ferocious and concentrated attack, completely destroyed the Syrian air defence complex of SAM missiles. In the aerial combat which ensured, as the Syrians desperately attempted to protect their ground installations, 29 MiG

Street fighting Two Israeli soldiers in action against the PLO along the street dividing East and West Beirut. The soldier on the left is falling after being hit by a PLO sniper.

The final phases Israeli M60 tanks being used as assault artillery during the last stages of the battle for Beirut. The signallers on the left are in touch with forward observers reporting the effect of fire.

PALESTINE

The hand-over Having fulfilled their mission in forcing the expulsion of PLO fighters from Beirut, the Israelis pulled back, allowing a UN force to take over the PLO evacuation. As if to underline Israeli success, this Merkava is parked outside PLO headquarters **(above)**. A French-manned Panhard armored car patrols **(right)**, while an Israeli M60 pulls back from the city center **(far right)**.

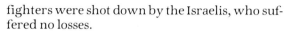

fighters were shot down by the Israelis, who suffered no losses.

That evening the Israelis again signalled to the Syrians, offering them the option of retiring, but they preferred to stay and fight it out, even moving new SA batteries and a brigade of T-72 tanks during the night. Next day the battle proper began, as Israeli armor moved forward, supported by the IAF, which was busy cutting supply routes behind the Syrians. One of the features of the battle was the first clashes between the new Israeli Merkava tank and the Syrian T-72s. In every case, the T-72 was destroyed.

On the coast, the ring around Beirut was complete and tightening, while mopping-up forces worked their way slowly through every village and town, clearing out nests of PLO fanatics and hauling out vast quantities of arms and ammunition from their hiding places. Thousands of tons of munitions were found, hundreds of terrorists captured, among them scores of foreign volunteers from some of the more notorious international terrorist groups.

Eventually, with all its objectives achieved, the Israeli government called a cease-fire on 11 June. This was frequently broken by the PLO and Syrian forces, so, finally on 22 June, the IDF mounted another major operation to clear out an enclave of Syrian and PLO troops on the Beirut-Damascus road. After three days, the remaining Syrians were allowed to withdraw into Syria and Operation 'Peace in Lebanon' finally came to an end.

Once again, United Nations' debate preceded the arrival of peace-keeping parties. For their part, the remnants of the PLO were allowed to evacuate Beirut, though without their weapons, for a variety of international destinations. The Israeli occupying forces now faced the invidious

The victors Israeli infantry in their armored personnel carriers roll through the streets of Beirut, having left the port area on the arrival of the peace-keeping force.

The vanquished An Israeli tank overlooks Beirut, alongside a political poster supporting the President of Lebanon **(above)**. The threat of renewed attack speeded PLO evacuation. A PLO guerrilla, with his belongings, is about to evacuate Beirut **(right)**; **(far right)** a pile of assorted weapons taken from PLO guerrillas.

task of holding down the areas of Lebanon they had occupied during the course of the operation. Not only were they doing this in the teeth of world opinion — this the Israelis have always been prepared to face. For the first time in Israel's history, voices were raised inside the country and the IDF about the wisdom of the move. Dissent reached a peak in the wake of the Beirut massacre of Palestinian refugees by Lebanese Christian militia, which the IDF did not nip in the bud, and the subsequent findings of an Israeli judicial investigation, which severely censured leading Israeli politicians and army leaders for their roles in the affair.

The story leading up to the massacres started in early September 1982. Israeli pressure had forced the evacuation of the active PLO forces from Beirut, and a degree of peace appeared to be within sight. Then, the President-elect of Lebanon, Bashir Gemayel, was assassinated. There were fears that this would trigger off all manner of reprisals and bloodshed within the Lebanese capital, and, as a precautionary measure, Israeli troops moved in and occupied the city.

A number of Palestinian refugee camps lay within the city limits and Israelis had little doubt that these were sheltering PLO terrorists, since their troops had come under sporadic gunfire from the camps' direction. So, on 16 September, the Israeli commanders authorised a force of Lebanese Christian Falangist troops to enter the

The massacre The Israeli policy of handing over control to the Lebanese Christian militia was to lead to the infamous Beirut camp massacre, though the Israelis disclaimed all responsibility. A squadron of militia tanks face the sea at Sidon **(above)**, while **(right)** Major Said Haddad, leader of the Christian militia, arrives at Beaufort Castle to take over command from Israeli forces.

camps and deal with these terrorist elements. The Falangists were chosen for several reasons. Firstly, the Israelis considered them to be more adept at distinguishing terrorists from genuine refugees; secondly, having completed their campaign, the Israelis were anxious to avoid further casualties of their own; and, thirdly, the employment of the Falangists would satisfy Israeli public opinion which felt that the former had not made sufficient contribution to the campaign.

Unfortunately the results of this seemingly logical operation were catastrophic. Some 700 to 800 people — men, women, children, terrorists, refugees, all suffered equally — were killed in the most brutal of circumstances. In two camps the Falangists entered, all the evidence showed that they simply set about systematically extermination all the occupants.

Apparently, little of this was known to the Israeli commanders at the time, although there appears to have been a degree of cynicism in the relations between the Falangists and the Israelis. On Friday 17 September, Lt-General Eitan, the Israeli Chief of Staff, met Falangist commanders in Beirut, during which, according to reports, he congratulated them on their operations to date and instructed them to continue clearing out the terrorists until the following day 'at which time they must stop, due to American pressure'. He also agreed to lend them a bulldozer to assist in 'removing illegal structures'. At 8am on the Saturday the Falangists left the camps, and shortly afterwards the full horror of their actions was revealed.

Once the world press and television began to spread the news of what had happened, the backlash against the Israeli army and government was enormous, while public opinion within Israel itself rapidly turned against Prime Minister Begin and his cabinet. After initially attempting to dismiss the reports of the massacres as a gross exaggeration, Begin was finally persuaded to set up an independent Commission of Enquiry which deliberated for several months before announcing its findings in February 1983.

From the Commission's report, it seemed that the significance of the Falangist involvement had been appreciated very early by the Deputy Prime Minister, David Levy. At a Cabinet meeting on 16 September, Minister of Defense Sharon and Eitan had casually mentioned the camp-clearing operation and had immediately been criticised by Levy: 'We could come out with no credibility when I hear that Falangists are already entering a certain neighbourhood; and I know what the meaning of revenge is for them, what kind of slaughter . . . Then no one will believe we went in to create order there, and we will bear the blame.' Accurate as his assessment was, the rest of the cabinet ignored his words.

The inquest Israeli involvement in Lebanon brought protests from Israelis themselves, particularly after the news of the Beirut camp massacre broke. Demonstrators in Tel Aviv **(top)** demand a cease-fire. President of the Supreme Court Yitzhak Kahan **(above)** headed the judicial enquiry into the massacre. This censured Defense Minister Ariel Sharon **(left)**, who was relieved of his post.

The Commission demanded Sharon's resignation and, had Eitan not been on the point of retiring, they would have demanded his as well. While it was acknowledged that Prime Minister Begin had little or no knowledge of the Falangist involvement, he was severly criticised for failing to make adequate enquiries and find out for himself what was going on. Evenutally, after some initial resistance, Sharon did resign, only to be offered a Ministry without Portfolio.

Above all else the Commission's report was concerned with the moral posture. 'The main purpose of the report', the commissioners stated, 'was to bring to light all the important facts relating to the perpetration of the atrocities; it therefore has importance from the perspective of Israel's moral fortitude and its functioning as a democratic state that scrupulously maintains the fundamental principles of the civilised world . . .' Without doubt the Commission did its utmost to discover the truth and allocate responsibility, even though the response of the Israeli government has seemed muted to many.

Index

Author's note
The arms business is now truly international. Given this, and the special position the Israelis occupy in the multi-national world, all technical specifications have been given as supplied by the Israeli Armed Forces, except where such information is classified by Israel itself.

Page numbers in *italic* **refer to captions and illustrations.**